The Seduction

Paul Francis is a director of *Going Public*, a church-based team that is committed not only to communicating the truths of the Christian faith in a relevant way, but also challenging people to live out their faith as a means of conveying God's love and concern for humanity.

He is a regular speaker on many subjects, including *The Seduction*. This is a multi-media tour which visits universities, schools and churches, exploring contemporary sexual issues from a Christian point of view.

The Seduction

Teenage sexuality – who's pulling the strings?

Paul Francis

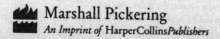

Marshall Pickering
An Imprint of HarperCollins*Publishers*

Marshall Pickering is an Imprint of
HarperCollins*Religious*
Part of HarperCollins*Publishers*
77–85 Fulham Palace Road, London W6 8JB

First published in Great Britain
in 1995 by Marshall Pickering

10 9 8 7 6 5 4 3 2 1

A catalogue record for this book is
available from the British Library

ISBN 0 551 02896-3

Typeset by Harper Phototypesetters Limited
Northampton, England
Printed and bound in Great Britain by
HarperCollinsManufacturing Glasgow

To dear Jane,
for loving me since the day we first met.
But above all, for constantly showing me the better way.

Contents

PART THREE
A Better Way to Live

Acknowledgements

In the past I have always skipped the acknowledgement section because I thought it was just a polite few words to thank a close circle of friends. Since writing this book I've come to realize that this is probably one of the most important pages in the book, for it is just a small reflection of all the hard work that many people have put in it. Without their time and effort it would not exist. These are some of the very special people who have helped.

Pat Brookes who read every word of the manuscript many times and made many helpful alterations. My good friend, Rob Parsons, who as always was there when I needed him.

To my colleague and friend, Joy, who never moaned at the amount of time this work kept me out of the office and who has given great support.

To my good friends, John Perkins, Mair Perkins, Claire West and Pat, who fought the 'other' battle that few know about but which made a huge difference.

To Anne Carlos, Jacqui Butler and Nick Bastable who all read the manuscript and made very helpful comments.

Thanks to my editor, Christine, who has been very patient with my offerings.

To Martyn Joseph, Pete Allison, Gaynor Thomas, Joy and members of Trapdoor Theatre Company who were there at the start of . . . *The Seduction*.

Finally to my best friend, Jane, who has patiently endured the long process of finishing this book.

Here and now I publicly say a heartfelt thank you to all of them. And if you enjoy and are helped by this book, you owe these people your thanks, too.

PART ONE

The Heart of the Seduction

one
Voices in the dark

Over the years I have spoken to many young people about sex. A constant theme that they talk to me about is the hurt that has been caused by the abuse and misunderstanding of sex. Below are just four of many comments I have heard. I call these voices in the dark.

'Please help me; I was abused when I was little and nobody knows about it.' *14-year-old*

'Thank you for all you've taught us,' she said. 'A few years ago I was really hurt by the misuse of sex and you've showed me that there is hope.' *16-year-old*

'Thanks for what you said this morning; it's too late for many of us. I wish that I had heard this stuff before!' *16-year-old*

'Is it true? Is it really possible? Can anybody really love me?' *17-year-old*

CHAPTER 1
Tattoo on the mind

Born to Lose

In the window were displayed samples of the tattoos available. On the chest or arms you could have tattooed an anchor or flag or mermaid or whatever. But what struck me with force were three words that you could choose to be tattooed on one's flesh. **Born to lose**

I entered the shop in astonishment and, pointing to those words, asked the Chinese tattoo artist, 'Does anyone really have that terrible phrase, **Born to lose***, tattooed on his body?'*

He replied, 'Yes, sometimes.'

'But,' I said, 'I just can't believe that anyone in his right mind would do that.'

The Chinese man simply tapped his forehead and said in broken English, 'Before tattoo on body, tattoo on mind!'[1]

'Before tattoo on body, tattoo on mind.' What a powerful concept! He is making the profound point that people will tattoo *born to lose* on their body because it's something they already believe in their minds. In other words, over the years everything that has been said to them, everything that has been done to them, every experience they've endured has said one thing – 'You're a loser!'

As I travel and talk with young people it is clear that more and more of them are acting as if they're born losers. You can tell it from the things they say, the look in their eyes, the body language, the way they wear their clothes. Every thing about them says, 'we are of little or no value'. To me it is one of the saddest indictments of our society. To have created a generation that has such a low opinion of itself is tragic. Why do young people act like that?

Simple. Their experience in life has already printed a clear message in their minds – you're a loser.

I recall one young man who came to talk with me. His eyes were full of tears as he told me his life story. A father who left home the day he was born. A mother who had a string of 'uncles' and who finally could not cope and so put her son in a home. He was fostered out a few times but kept going back to the home. And now at the age of seventeen he sat at the back of a hall and asked, 'Are you really sure that God loves me? Are you really sure? Is it possible?' He could not comprehend how anybody could love him when all his life had tattooed one message on his mind – 'nobody cares for you, nobody loves you, you're a loser'.

An exception, you say. The circumstances may be although I would contend that they are more common than we care to admit. But the truth is universal – the tattoos on our mind affect who we are. Young people absorb life around them, learning through each of their senses. The tattoos we leave on their minds are of profound importance. This book is about sex, but it's more than that. It's about the systems that affect all of us – it's about the battle for our children's bodies, minds and spirits.

Modern society is very different from that just thirty years ago. So much has changed in terms of science, technology, travel, money, industry and family life. Some of this change is for the good, some, however, is for the worse. But more disturbing is the change in the moral structures – what people consider of value and worth. It's this change which is leaving the major tattoos on our minds.

Don't despair, though, for this book is about hope.

We can change the forces that affect us.

We can give people value and dignity.

We can feel loved again because the fundamental point of this book is that . . . *there is a better way for us to live.*

I hope that together we can enter into the joy and pain, the pressures and the freedom of the young. I hope we can see that there are no easy or simple answers. There will be much pain and sacrifice. But if we dare to take up the challenge of *the better way*, if we will take a few risks – it is possible to change the tattoos.

CHAPTER 2
Is there any hope?

It's a Monday morning and I'm in a school hall that begins to bustle with life as children make their way in. They are excited because this is something different – and anything has to be better than double chemistry! They are coming to *The Seduction . . . the lie about sex.* This is a fast-moving multi-media presentation we've developed to look at the issues surrounding sex. For the next three hours through the medium of drama, music, speech and large-screen video we will look at the pressures young people face. Love, self-worth, sex, pregnancy and AIDS will all be tackled. But now I stand in front of 300 young people and ask them a simple question:

How many of you think that sexual intercourse should only be experienced within marriage?

As I look at 300 stunned faces one brave young girl tentatively raised her hand. As she did so the sniggers began from her so-called friends. I continued with another question:

Would you consider it a compliment to be called a virgin?

Not even the one brave girl had enough courage to put her hand up at this point. The sniggers and jeers of her 'friends' had seen to that. My final question really got them:

How many of you believe living with the same person for the rest of your life is possible?

Again not a single hand went up but this time the sniggers had turned to laughter.

The Seduction presentation has been seen by thousands all over Great Britain. Every time I look out over those young faces that have experienced so much of 'life', I ask myself a question. How has this change in values taken place? How have we raised a generation who find these questions a joke?

As I travel to many schools all around the country it is becoming increasingly clear that the concept of sex outside marriage is normal, that the concept of marriage is very negative and that sex is a commodity which can be used like any other object.

Please don't get me wrong; I'm not against sex. Far from it, I think it is a wonderful gift. In fact whenever I speak on the subject I always start with the statement: 'I think sex is great!'

After saying it I can guarantee that two reactions will take place. First, it will silence everybody. Second, there will be a look of shock on many faces. The shock is not because I am talking about sex; in all probability they know more about it than I do! Rather the shock occurs because they have put me in the 'religious' bracket. And their perception of 'religious' people is they don't enjoy anything – let alone sex! Well, I have good news for them and for you. We are meant to enjoy sex; it's one of God's gifts to us. He intends that we should enjoy it to the maximum within the framework He gave.

Sex is great

I am making that statement right at the beginning of this book so that you understand where I am coming from. I want people to enjoy sex to the full. The trouble is that we are living in a culture that's projecting an unreal image of sex. Sex is great, but it's certainly not what life is all about. For example, I believe it's possible to live a life without having sex and be totally fulfilled. It's hard to believe that is possible with all the lies about this subject: lies that equate sex with love and acceptance; lies that project sex to be the ultimate fulfilment and risk free. They are lies which put enormous pressure on all of us, and which make us feel like second class citizens if we are not in a regular sexual relationship; lies which put enormous pressure on young people to have sex before they are ready – lies that are creating . . . the seduction.

My message is simple. I appreciate the frustrations of living a life of saying no to sex until you are in a lifelong relationship. I realize that for some that relationship may never come and therefore it commits them to a life of abstinence. That is hard. I do believe, however, that God's frameworks for life are liberating and not enslaving. The hope for our lives is not another sex partner; rather it's resting in the security and knowledge that we are loved and of great value . . .

The cries from the heart

I remember going to one school and at the end of a day a note was slipped to me. It simply read: 'Please help me; I was abused when I was little and nobody knows about it.'

In another school a 16-year-old girl came to me, tears streaming down her face. 'Thank you for all you've taught us,' she said. 'A few years ago I was really hurt by the misuse of sex and you've showed me that there is hope.'

Another boy got to the heart of the issue, 'Thanks for what you said this morning; it's too late for many of us. I wish that I had heard this stuff before!'

There are countless lives that are broken and damaged because they have not had all the facts about sex and relationships. Children, teenagers, indeed all of us have the right to have all the information so that we can make informed choices. This book is arguing that saying no to sex until one is married is a positive choice. We want to affirm the belief in virginity, as something *positive*. We also want to affirm second virginity. This recognizes that people are now sexually active but may want to change. They can and do. The principles are still the same. It's called second virginity because it's as if you started again. To tell a child that saying no is a positive choice is to give that child freedom.

Simply telling young people about the reproduction process and contraception is not enough. There is already a wealth of information on the subject. Nor is it realistic to simply tell them that abstinence is a positive choice. Above all they need to be informed about the value and dignity of relationships. They need to be told that they are loved. I have spoken to thousands of teenagers about love and self-worth and as I speak I can sense they desperately want to believe it. There is something within all of us that can only be satisfied when we rest in the security of knowing that we are precious and loved. What our culture needs is not more sex education, but love education.

CHAPTER 3
What's really going on?

So what is the problem? What are young people doing? Is it of any consequence? What are the changing trends in sexual behaviour? These are big questions, but all the research shows that there is a great concern for the trends regarding sexual practices of young people – teenage pregnancies and sexually-transmitted diseases are increasing.

According to Professor Francis and Dr Kay who surveyed 15,361 British children aged between 13 to 15, only one in seven thinks that sex outside of marriage is morally wrong. Fewer than 25 per cent have any qualms about the idea of having sex under the legal age of sixteen.[2]

Only one in five thinks that there is anything wrong with divorce. Over half think that divorce is perfectly acceptable simply when a relationship turns sour.

In 1991, one study showed that 41 per cent of young people claim to have had sexual intercourse before the age of sixteen. At sixteen the percentage rises to 52 per cent and by the age of twenty, 88 per cent have had intercourse.[3]

In 1993, 661,261 people were seen in NHS clinics suffering from a sexually-transmitted disease. 51.3 per cent of these were under the age of twenty-five. 17.2 per cent were teenagers.[4]

The World Health Organization (WHO) estimates that by the year 2000, 10 million children will have an HIV infection, and another 10 million will have had a parent who has died because of HIV. With 1 in 250 of the entire global population already infected, and with one new person being infected every fifteen seconds, this is not a problem which will go away.[5]

In a Health Education survey of 4,000 young people aged 16 to

9, 25 per cent indicated that they would be willing to have unprotected sex with a new partner and only 34 per cent felt that they needed to change their lifestyles because of AIDS.

What about church based young people?

When I'm speaking at a church youth meeting it is not unusual for the church pastor or one of the leaders to have a quiet word with me before I speak. 'We're glad you're speaking on sex. Mind you, it's probably a bit of a waste of your time as it's not a problem here.'

I have been to colleges and universities where members of the Christian Union executive have considered speaking on the subject a waste of time as sex is not a problem. Such views amaze me. The only explanation for them is that people do not want to face the issues.

To examine this problem a survey was carried out in 1991 by Marc Europe and Agape UK which examined teenage sexual activities and attitudes in the Church. The sample included all major denominations as well as the 'new' churches.[6] The results were disturbing in that they found the difference between secular and Christian young people was narrowing.

According to this survey in the 13 to 19 age bracket, 18 per cent of them responded that they had had sexual intercourse. Further more by the age of nineteen this figure had risen to 43 per cent.

These statistics are alarming enough, but what is more disturbing is the response to another set of questions. The first set of questions dealt with action and behaviour. The survey, however, asked a second set of questions about attitudes – what they believe about issues. They wanted to discover what the young people thought was right and wrong. The 13 to 16 age bracket were asked the following question:

'For two people who are not married but both willing, which of the following are morally acceptable?'

A list of possibilities followed: holding hands, fondling of breasts and so on – the last one being sexual intercourse. Thirty one per cent of 13 to 16-year-olds thought that sexual intercourse was all right if both partners consented. Another question asked how many respondents had had sexual intercourse. In the 13 to 16 age bracket, one in five responded that they were having sexual intercourse. That means in a youth group of sixty, twelve of the 13 to 16-year-olds are likely to have had sexual intercourse. But it gets worse. The same age group were asked a question about attitude. What was tattooed on their mind? One in three thought that sexual intercourse was morally acceptable if both partners were consenting. So one third of 13 to 16-year-olds in your church youth group will consider that sexual activity at their age is normal.

These findings are disturbing because the tattoos we leave on the mind of the young today will become their actions tomorrow.

It is no wonder that all these statistics led Sarah Strickland of *The Independent* to write:

> The need is becoming more pressing, not less. Unplanned pregnancies are increasing, and more teenagers than ever are having sex, often without using contraception. HIV infection is becoming more frequent among young people; and they are not changing their sexual behaviour to protect themselves.[7]

Behind these statistics are real people. People who have feelings and emotions, and lives that are hurting and broken. Contrary to a lot of reports we are not creating more freedom for young people, but a mountain of broken and disillusioned lives. What has possessed us to do this to our young? Where did we leave the rails?

Because the teenage years are difficult enough, of all the periods in life this is the one for giving protection and security. Instead young people are left to the exploitation of advertising agencies and large international companies. We have created a culture of images that promise them so much but delivers so little. Far from liberating people our present culture is enslaving them.

I hope that the next few chapters will help as we begin to look at the problem and some of the issues and possible ways forward. You may be a parent or a youth leader who is struggling to deal with this whole area with your teenagers. I hope that you will find the book helpful in giving you some insights into some of the pressures that today's teenagers are under. I also hope that by the end you will have resources that will help you deal more positively with the subject.

Summary

- The tattoos left on children's minds will affect their perception of themselves.
- Sex is a good gift from God.
- Saying no to sexual intercourse is a positive choice. To deny the person the option is to deny their freedom.
- Behind all the statistics are real and often suffering people.

two
The tattoo-makers

I won't be here in the next century doing this job, but I think there will be a problem; I think our children will be assaulted from all sides; they will have televisions in their room by then, probably video, probably satellite dishes attached to those televisions so they will see everything. *We must somehow give them the strength to resist . . . I think it's a matter of survival not only for the individual but also for society.*[8]
James Ferman, British Board of Film Classifier

I believe that television changes society. I think we have already changed it, and there are some things that we've done which I regret. Television has been responsible for producing or adding to an ethos of covetousness. We have become more grasping. *Aubrey Singer*

One prime objective of all advertising is to heighten expectations. To create the illusion that the product or service will perform the miracles you expect. *Al Ries*

CHAPTER 4
The image-makers

In 1989 a group called Milli Vanilli released their first record, *Girl, you know it's true*. It was a massive hit and sold 7 million copies. They won the 1989 Grammy Award for the best new album and were regarded as a major new talent. However, just six months after achieving this it was discovered that they did not sing or play on the record. A record producer had a 'sound' that he wanted to sell but not the image. He therefore found some people who looked good and put them on the video. The fact that they could not sing nor play a single musical note was not important – what he needed was an image of someone who looked good – their image would do the rest and sell the sound!

This is a perfect example of the culture we have created for young people. It is a culture that constantly produces images and sells them as truth. Images are created and we are told that they are within our grasp. Some are cold, deliberate distortions, others not so. The result is the same – a culture that believes in the image. All we need do is to reach out and touch them. Dreams and aspirations are manipulated so that a given product promises to make them come true.

Don't get me wrong; I'm all for dreams. I remember that when I was a little boy I wanted to be a pilot. The thought of flying off to all those exotic locations was heaven to me. I would dream of sitting in the pilot's seat and pressing the throttle as we went for take-off. I would dream of heroics. The plane was on a collision course with the Empire State Building, and owing to my exceptional bravery and skill I would always save the day.

I am one of millions of children who used to dream that one day we would be pilots, footballers, musicians, doctors or nurses. All of

17

us as children have had the dreams, if you like, the belief in the images. Soon however we grow up to the 'big' world and we learn the truth of childhood dreams. Working as a doctor is good and it's fun. But people do die and you don't always find the miracle cure. Being a pilot is a good job, but planes sometimes crash. In other words we develop a much rounder picture as we discover reality.

Here I'm not referring to those childhood dreams and images. The image-making that concerns me is the more cynical distortion of the truth which slowly corrupts the minds of all of us. The kings of image-making are the advertising agencies and the media.

Selling the image

I have a problem in life – I can never find jeans that fit! I can find jeans that fit my waist, but then I can't get my backside in! I can find jeans that accommodate my behind but are four inches too long on the leg. What man has not spent a wet Saturday getting more frustrated by the hour as he can't find anything that fits? How many groans and sighs are heard from shops' changing rooms as we all try to make clothes fit? Women discover they are a size 10 above the waist, 12 round it and 14 beneath it. Try to find a dress that fits that!

The problem is that we have been sold the image. We look at the glossy adverts and the clothes look so good but above all they fit. We know it's true – be honest, how many of us have tried clothes on only to complain that they look nothing like the way the model shows them?

We should not condemn ourselves – rather we should realize two things about adverts. First, the models they use do not have typical body shapes. The models have body shapes which are the exception as opposed to the norm. Nevertheless even models have the clothes fitted specially so that they 'fit' in all the right places. Clothes are made to fit the model. They use pins and clips to pull the cloth in at the right place. It is an image.

Second, I never forget the day I received proofs from the printers for a new brochure we were planning. The proofs included a photograph of me! It is a fair observation that I never particularly like photographs of myself. To my surprise I liked the one on the

ew publicity. I telephoned the designer and asked if he had a few
spare that we could use for other work. His reply was a classic: 'Yes,
you can have a few,' he told me, 'but you need to realize that we've
touched them up'! Using computer technology he was able to
change the colour of my skin, take away the double chin and give
me a thinner face. No wonder I liked it!

That is the power of the 'touch up' artist who can, with his
computer and chemicals, remove wrinkles from photographs, take
away the double chin or that slightly bulging stomach. They can
make you look any way you want – in other words they are image-
makers.

The trouble is that we buy into the image. We believe that we
should have the bodies that we see on the adverts selling clothes.
The model shape is the norm by which we judge everything else.
That is the power of advertising. This is summed up by Al Ries
and Jack Trout in *Positioning: The Battle for Your Mind*:

> One prime objective of all advertising is to heighten
> expectations. To create the illusion that the product or
> service will perform the miracles you expect.[9]

The adverts promise teenagers that 'zits' can be got rid of by
purchasing their facial wash. Furthermore, pre-facial wash you had
plenty of 'zits' but no girls; post-facial wash, however, and no 'zits'
– hey presto, an armful of girls. It is the media which is able to
create an image – if we buy their product it will satisfy some desire
deep within us. It is the media which portray the Gordon Geckos
of this world as if they were real achievers. Gordon Gecko was the
star of the film *Wall Street* and one can still hear his haunting
speech which finished with the words, 'Greed is good'. And the
image is such that we believe it – despite the ending, we are left
feeling that the Gordon Geckos of this world are the real winners.
It is the image-making that sells us great political truths in five-
minute sound-bites.

It is the image-making that is cynical and cruel because it is
targeted at our hearts. All of us, at the centre of our being, crave for
acceptance, friendship and peace of mind. Adverts blatantly
exploit these needs by claiming to meet our greatest spiritual and

19

emotional needs: cigars to meet our need for peace of mind, lager to meet our deepest need for companionship and the greatest of them all is Coca-Cola which will meet our deepest need for love.

The seducing power of advertising

Adverts, at their core, offer the buyer an image of himself that's made more glamorous by the products they are trying to sell. They suggest that if he buys what they are offering, his life will become much better. The adverts show people in houses that we envy, wearing clothes we would like to own and driving cars we only dream of. But the adverts promise us that they can be ours. But it's more than that; they seduce us with their products. And the greatest ingredient in this seduction? Sex.

Sex sells. Magazines know it and advertisers know it. You can't open a magazine or watch an advert on television without sex having some part. A woman's body is used to sell everything from deodorant to luggage. More and more the male form is being exploited as well.

Mind you, not everybody is happy about it. So far the Club 18–30 adverts have been banned after 430 people complained about their sexy imagery; the Häagen-Dazs campaign has provoked 80 complaints; the Wonderbra posters caused forty people to send written complaints, and the post is rolling in since the advertisement for the film *Disclosure*, featuring Demi Moore pressing up against Michael Douglas, was released.

Are the adverts fair to women? Are they projecting the right image? Opinion is divided on the subject. Ann Mayne from the Campaign Against Pornography believes that modern advertising has put women's rights back decades. She observed:

> Pornography is becoming part of High Street culture. And women cannot be empowered when the images used are degrading and oppressive.

Others do not agree. Aven Carole, from Feminists Against Censorship, says:

> *Disclosure* is about a sexually aggressive woman and the
> poster is therefore appropriate to the subject. Images like
> these are not going to ruin women's lives; there are more
> important issues to debate. Sexual attitudes existed before
> these images were around. All they are doing is showing that
> nice girls are allowed to be sensual creatures as well.[10]
> (*Daily Express*, 7 March, 1995, p.20)

While agreeing that the issues are not simple, I also recognize
that women may feel that it is simply representing their true sexuality. I do, however, question the assumption that the images in
adverts are harmless. Many youngsters tell me that they do buy
into the images. They believe the hype.

Below are two examples of adverts that show how sex is abused.

Advert 1

It was a full-page advertisement in all the 'heavy' papers. The page
was blue and made to look like the European Community flag.
But instead of twelve flags representing the twelve members of
the Community there were twelve condoms. The large caption
read:

> *Inter-Rail. You've got the rest of your life to be good.*
> The Inter-Rail Pass gives you the freedom to go as far
> as you want in Europe.

The inference of the advert was simple – you are young; enjoy
yourself before it's too late.

Next, here is some evidence that sometimes the advertisers' use
of sex in advertising is not only inappropriate but also laughable.

Advert 2

'I am the Chinaman,' he said, and brushed his fingers against *my*
face, *gently*. A pulse of electricity charged the tiny hairs at the back
of my neck as my mouth opened instinctively; his head close to
mine, this man, this powerful, strong-limbed stranger from the
East. Caught in his embrace, I felt exhilarated; consumed with my
own desires for the first time since Paulo. *Slowly*, his mouth

21

caressed the soft skin of my forehead, my eyes, my face. My lips craved his. *'Feed me'*, they screamed as he clasped my hair and threw me down on to the bed. I drew him down after me, hungrily, tearing at his shirt. The heat of his kisses washed over me like a great wave. Fingers of fire moved instinctively over my skin. The silk sheets rucked beneath our bodies as he removed my underclothing with one masterful stroke of his arm; my breath caught in my throat as *I felt his* Low Fat, Golden Wonder Pot Light Chinese Chicken Flavour. *So tasty,* so filling, it's more satisfying than a stolen moment of forbidden lust in the heart of Red China, and it's got fewer than 200 calories. *Intense.*

Computers – great invention

The screen is no bigger than 6 in. × 6 in. but through it I can link up with any data-bank in the world. I can talk with my bank, book an air ticket and soon I shall be able to order clothes. The power of a computer is awesome. There is no doubt they are a great invention. They are making a huge difference to all our lives. Much of it is for good, but there are dangers. Unfortunately a few people have realized the potential for making a fortune at the expense of our children. Computer pornography is becoming a major problem. In a recent study 50 per cent of the 8,500 schools involved admitted that computer pornography had been available to their pupils, some as young as eight.[11]

For 99p you can buy hard-core pornographic computer disks. *The Independent* newspaper bought some and reported:

> Disks advertised in one of Britain's most widely read computer magazines, showed scenes of anal intercourse, ejaculation into a woman's mouth, and two men simultaneously penetrating a woman.[12]

The article went on to say:

> Many parents would be surprised that pornography was available on disk and horrified that it could cost only 99p. The disks are not even labelled as pornographic and they look like any other disk.

Disks are now available that give you choice. By the 'click' of the computer mouse you can decide how a woman is to be stripped. You have a choice of what sexual acts are to be carried out. You are now in control!

Unfortunately the problem does not stop there as now we have the 'electronic highway'. This development means that anyone with a computer and a telephone can link up to any bank of information in the world. For a small joining fee the world's information is at your fingertips. The potential for development is awesome, but equally though the potential for misuse is frightening. Any child with access to a computer will be able to link into pornographic material and at the moment there is no control. The future may seem dark, but there is hope. There is a better way to live. And the good news is that more people are becoming disillusioned with the way things are and they too want to find this better way. Hang in there!

CHAPTER 5
Telly addicts

The average lifespan of a human being is seventy years. It is in truth a very short time. It goes before we realize it. When we are young we think that our time on earth goes on for ever. However, as we grow older we realize that too is an image – time goes by. Imagine then, that somebody came to you and asked the following questions. What would you do if you were given an extra month to live? What would you do if you were given an extra year to live? What would you do if you were given an extra eight years to live? Imagine those eight years. What would you do with them? Work harder? Spend more time with the family? Who knows, but what is amazing is that it is not a hypothetical question. We can have the extra eight years and all we have to do is to stop watching television! By the time the average person is seventy they will have spent eight of those years watching television. Stop watching it and you free up the best part of a decade!

Television and now video are two of the most powerful forces in moulding our present thinking. They have become one of the great shapers of human perception. They have the ability to produce and push images into every household and convince us that they are true. You can't walk into any sports shop, department store, restaurant or bar without finding television screens hanging everywhere pumping out the images.

The average person watches 3.2 hours of television a day. In one week 23 hours are spent watching television.

In *The United Kingdom 1991* 98 per cent (Britain 1987, C.O.I.) of households have a television set, 36 per cent have two and 58 per cent own a video.

Children's access to television has increased dramatically with lmost a fifth of households having a television set in their children's bedroom.

Fifty per cent of families with children aged ten to fifteen had a et in the bedroom as well as a main set, as did 36 per cent of families with 5 to 8-year-olds.

Ninety per cent of homes with children have a video recorder, 3 per cent of families have a computer and 17 per cent of homes with children have satellite television.[13]

This power can be used for good or evil and there is no doubt hat a lot of television is good. It is openly acknowledged that 3ritish television is the best in the world. Some of our 'soaps' can make powerful social comments. For example *Eastenders'* treatment of the AIDS issue was excellent. Some drama productions uch as *Middlemarch* and *GBH* won countless prizes. Nobody questions the professionalism of our television industry, but neither lare we question the power of the box.

The power of the box

A few years ago a *News at Ten* producer was watching a late-night elevision documentary on Channel 4. The programme showed a tarving child in Africa which so moved this producer that he lecided to show the clip on the following evenings news. Bob Geldof was watching the news and he was so moved by the image hat he decided that something must be done to help the starving. And out of that one image came *Live Aid* and *Band Aid* which aised over fifty million pounds for the third world.

There is no doubt the media has a lot of power which can be used for both good and evil. Who exercises this power? Who lecides what can be shown, what is important and what needs to be highlighted? Who is setting the agenda? What values do these beople have? Some would say that producers are value-free in that hey do not allow what they believe to affect what they make, but hat is not the case. For instance it is obvious that Oliver Stone's xperience in Vietnam is reflected in his material. Our view and philosophy of life will be reflected in the way we say and do things. There is nothing wrong with this; we just need to be aware that it akes place. What we say and do is influenced by who we are.

That is why there is great concern in this country that the owner ship of newspapers is falling into the hands of a few people who have the money to buy them. Many recognize that the power to set the agendas is falling into fewer and fewer hands. Whatever the political persuasion of newspaper owners, that tendency has to be dangerous

An example of 'who we are' influencing a programme can be seen in a programme that most consider to be neutral – the news. The most important story is always the first. Subsequent stories are important, but there is the sense that the longer the news goes on the less important is the story.

Now try a little test: for the next few days watch the main news on BBC and ITV. You will probably discover that the main news story will be the same on both channels (though this is not always the case), but subsequent items will vary from channel to channel. Ask yourself why this is. Why do news stories vary from channel to channel? One of the reasons is that BBC and ITV have different influences. ITV is a commercial company and needs to raise its revenue through advertising. The news, like any other programme, has to win viewers. This must affect the way that the news is chosen and presented. The BBC on the other hand is paid for by you and me and therefore it has a duty to us. This again must affect the way it presents the news. Furthermore a team of people has to decide which story goes first, which news to cover and which story is pertinent. The values and beliefs these people hold will affect that judgement.

As an example, a couple of years ago a tabloid newspaper ran the headline, 'Freddie Starr ate my hamster'. Whatever the merits of the story I would suggest that there were far more newsworthy items around. The problem is that somebody somewhere decided that was the most important story to run with. On what basis was that decision made and who had responsibility for it?

Two big lies about television

Lie 1: It presents things as they are

During the 1992 general election the Conservative Party ran an advert on television called, 'The Journey'. It was a powerful piece of advertising because it had one message at the centre – John Major is one of us. It showed John Major being driven back to his ld neighbourhood, walking in the local market, meeting the people and talking about the changes that had taken place since he had left. Finally it showed him going back to the house where he grew up. The message was simple but very powerful – I'm one of you.

That advert for me crystallizes the type of culture we live in – we live in a culture which creates images. What the Conservative Party was selling was an image and the image was – 'John Major is one of us'. The truth however, is that John Major is not one of us. He cannot be – he has moved on. As Prime Minister of this country he now has people who plan every minute of the day. He has people who drive him wherever he wants to go; he has a helicopter at his disposal. He has power. This does not make him any better or worse than you or me, but it certainly means that he is not one of 'us'. Yet the image-makers try to make us believe it is so. They are creating an image to hide the truth. Politics is now sold to us in five-minute video bites. It is no longer an issue of beliefs or manifestos; it is simply one of image. So we are encouraged to vote for the politician who has the right advertising agency to create the 'right' image. And what about truth? What is truth? Who cares anymore anyway?

The author and media-watcher Len Masterman recognized the problem when he said:

> For those who control and work in the media do not simply
> have the power to set agendas, provide explanations and
> construct their own version of events. They have a much
> more significant power to project these things as natural
> and authentic – simply part of the way things are.[14]

It is simply not true to say that television tells it the way it really is. Television is in essence the world interpreted for us. I will never forget the brilliant film *Broadcast News* starring William Hurt. In it he portrayed a man who wanted to be the anchorman on the main news programme. The whole tenor of the film was simple – the news is not important, but rather the way that it is presented. There was one chilling moment when William Hurt was shown on camera being made to cry by a very moving life

story. However, the truth was revealed in that the story did no
move him. Rather he had the ability to make himself cry at wil
This was filmed and then inserted into the main story. Howeve
the television audience did not see this; they were led to believ
that the story made him cry. We are led to believe that's the way i
was.

Lie 2: Television represents life

A popular argument is that television reflects life. If programme
are more violent, if there is more swearing and sex that's onl
because it's representing life. The argument does have som
validity. But to look at it in detail, let us examine some viewin
figures.

Millions of viewers in the week ending 25 December, 1994

BBC1		ITV	
1 Eastenders (Tue.)	15.58	1 Coronation St (Mon.)	17.68
2 Casualty	15.21	2 Coronation St (Fri.)	17.6.
3 Eastenders (Thu.)	15.15	3 Coronation St (Wed.)	16.48
4 One Foot in the Grave	15.14	4 Christmas Heartbeat	13.79
5 National Lottery	15.07	5 The Bill	13.79

Those figures reveal a number of things. First, a lot of peop
watch television. In fact the television has become anoth
member of the household. One of the results of this is that many
us would not know how to live without it. Furthermore, there is
perception that we've always lived this way and that we've alway
had television, but obviously this is not the case. People lived an
enjoyed life without television for thousands of years. We wou
survive without it. Television has only become a regular memb
of the household in the last thirty-five years.

Second, the overwhelming majority of the top programmes a
soaps – very well made soaps at that. They are well crafted an
enjoyable programmes, but they do not represents life. *Eastender*
The Bill, *Coronation Street* and a whole host of other programme
may be very good television, but they are not life. Certainly the
contain all the elements of life, but it is an interpretation of lif

Even when we have 'fly on the wall' documentaries, there is an element of unreality because people will always react differently when a camera is around.

During 1994, *The Daily Mail*, decided to find out if television really was a reflection of life. They monitored the four main television channels and recorded all the acts of violence on show. The following is a typical cross-section of the week's viewing beginning on Tuesday 9 March with *The Bill*:

Tuesday: Three hooded robbers wielding pickaxe handles burst into a petrol station, smash it up and attack the owner who arms himself with a stick. A body is shown being hit in close-up and a bystander is kicked in the groin.

Wednesday: 10.00p.m. (The Movie Channel), *Friday the 13th, Part III:* A woman is stabbed in the neck with a knitting needle which emerges from the mouth. She is one of twelve victims to lose their lives in this gratuitously violent film.

Friday: 9.30p.m. (BBC2), *Arena*: Shocking sexual violence as a man sits on a chair over a trussed-up woman whom he appears to be keeping as his sex slave; 'Like a donkey, do what I say,' he tells her. 'Ride and beat – you're the same.' We hear her screams, but cannot see her being beaten and possibly raped. This is the implication, however, portrayed by another man listening outside.

Sunday: 10.10p.m. (Channel 4), *The Krays*: Despite worries about the level of violence in one of the most brutal films for years, Channel 4 decided to give the story of the terrible twins' reign of gangland terror its television première. The sickening scenes in this production overshadow anything else shown that night. We see Ronnie Kray confront a man wielding a flick knife behind a London club. He persuades him to drop the weapon, pretending that the matter is settled. Then Kray pulls out a bayonet, places it across the man's mouth and pushes until blood pours. In mocking tones, the gangster says that he has given his victim a permanent smile.

At a snooker hall a vicious brawl erupts in which one man is slashed with a knife and a number of others are beaten up. Finally the Krays pin a man to a snooker table and plunge a sword through his hand. Towards the end of the film, rogue Kray gang member Jack 'the Hat' McVitie tries to escape a hit squad by smashing a head through a window. He is dragged back and Ronnie plunges a knife into his face with McVitie's blood spattering him.

One week of monitoring television violence tells you that it's not a true reflection of life. In only seven days the toll of carnage and chaos was: 401 killings, 119 woundings with guns, knives or other weapons, 188 brawls, 29 instances of foul and aggressive language and 27 of sexual violence. Satellite TV is more violent with 193 killings on Sky Movies Plus and 96 on The Movie Channel.

In the average week 14 people are killed in Britain.

Four hundred and one killings on television and 14 in real life. Television does not reflect life. Programmes such as *Eastenders* and *Casualty* are life condensed into 30 and 50 minutes respectively. *Casualty* takes what happens in a day in the average life of a hospital and condenses it into one 50-minute programme. The power of television is in its ability to make the extreme seem ordinary.

CHAPTER 6

Does what we watch affect who we are?

It is a very important question that causes great debate. Only one movie or TV show may not have a major effect on a life; rather it is the accumulated effects of negative images that occur hour by hour, day by day, week in week out. The issue is not so much the effect of one film here and another there. Rather it is the insidious erosion of values as we take in week by week the messages put out by the soaps and by adverts. To sit and watch advert after advert which reinforce the values of materialism over everything else must alter our perception of what is of value. I believe that television changes our behaviour for a number of reasons:

Reason 1: Advertisers believe it

Advertising is powerful. Just think how some of its advertising slogans have stayed with you. Try this little test: below is a series of catch-phrases; see if you can remember the product:

> Vorsprung durch Technik, as they say in Germany[15]
> It's good to talk[16]
> Don't die of ignorance[17]
> Once smitten . . .[18]
> I bet he drinks . . .[19]

See it works!

Companies spend millions of pounds a year selling their product because they believe that the cumulative effect changes shopping behaviour.

During the Rugby World Cup advertisers reputedly spent £100,000 a minute to promote their products. Barclays are alleged to have made a commercial with Ridley Scott that cost £250,000. Furthermore, they spent another £1,060,000 on screening it an average of twice a day in each ITV region.

Tesco apparently spent £50 million on an advertising campaign which featured Dudley Moore looking for chickens. In the process of trying to find these chickens he toured the world finding new products for Tesco to sell.

In 1991 Sainsburys launched a new advertising campaign which featured well-known celebrities demonstrating new recipes. The effect of the campaign was immediate. Selina Scott talked about pasta, the result of which was that Sainsburys sold six months' supply of Mozzarella cheese in one week. John Nettles, the actor who played *Bergerac*, went on about pepperoni and Sainsburys sold seven times its normal volume. And so their campaign went on. According to Sainsbury research, in the weeks after the recipe advertisement for a fish dish with limes was aired, each night 150,000 households sat down to eat it.

By combining classic music tracks with their new product, Levis were able to turn around their fortunes. Gold Blend sales went up 15 per cent when they aired their soap opera-style commercials.

Reason 2: Research suggests it's true

In 1993 Walt Disney chiefs were forced to cut a scene from their new film owing to a spate of children copying part of the action. The programme showed drunken college football players trying to prove their manhood by lying head to toe in the middle of a busy highway as cars rushed by.

Eighteen-year-old Michael Shingledecker, who saw the film was a week later killed by a truck as he lay on a highway dividing line. Seventeen-year-old Dean, who was hit by the same truck, was critically injured. In another incident a 17-year-old boy from New York was hit and critically injured while lying in the middle of the street. The driver of the car reported as having seen about fifty young people standing by the roadside.

The writer and director of the film, David Ward, said:

While the scene in no way advocated this irresponsible

activity, it is impossible for us to ignore that someone may have recklessly chosen to imitate it.

Writing in the journal of the American Medical Association, Dr Rothenburg, who works at Seattle's Children's Orthopaedic Hospital and Medical Centre, said that fifty studies involving 10,000 children and adolescents from every conceivable background all showed that viewing violence produces increased aggressive behaviour in the young.

Professor Inga Soneson spent ten years monitoring the lives of 200, 6 to 16-year-olds and the effect of television. Her research showed that among boys in particular there was a pronounced correlation between emotional disturbance and intensive television and video viewing. Boys who spent long periods in front of the television as 6-year-olds developed more aggression than their contemporaries. She went on to comment:

> When I began the research project, I had a positive attitude towards children and television. Today I strongly question whether a civilized society can condone children watching extreme violence.

In 1994 a report appeared which was based on a comprehensive survey of more than 1,000 teachers nationwide. The report was compiled by Jackie Miller, Deputy General Secretary of the Professional Association of Teachers. Her conclusion was:

> The message from this survey is that the problem is not confined to the small number of extremely disturbed children who sit at home watching violent videos like *Driller Killer*. The much greater problem is the effect of TV, computer games and videos on the vast majority of children. They are getting enormous and frequent exposure to unsuitable – often adult – material and it is having a very serious impact on their behaviour.

Let me finish this chapter with some quotes from some people in the media. They should know!

I won't be here in the next century doing this job, but I think there will be a problem; I think our children will be assaulted from all sides; they will have televisions in their room by then, probably video, probably satellite dishes attached to those televisions so they will see everything. *We must somehow give them the strength to resist . . . I think it's a matter of survival not only for the individual but also for society.*[20] *James Ferman, British Board of Film classifier*

I believe that television changes society. I think we have already changed it, and there are some things that we've done which I regret. Television has been responsible for producing or adding to an ethos of covetousness. We have become more grasping. *Aubrey Singer*

I began increasingly to become aware of the limitations and dangers of television; that it was a medium of shock rather than explanation; that it was a crude medium which strikes at the emotions rather than the intellect. And because of its insatiable appetite for visual actions, and for violence very often, it tended to distort and trivialize . . . it has contributed to the spate of unreason and violence and conflict in our society.[21] *Sir Robin Day*

It is actively in people's conscious and unconscious minds. Willy-nilly, *Coronation Street* and *The Sweeney* and the values these programmes transmit touch a reciprocal value system in people. So TV is constantly managing popular values. It's saying: Of course you have these values and of course they're right.[22] *Roland Joffe*

According to data gathered, pre-school children watch thirty hours of TV a week. Educators and experts in child development suggest that more than ten hours a week can have a detrimental effect on children's attention span, communication skills and creative abilities.[23]

CHAPTER 7
The battle for the box

most homes a new-born baby is first introduced to the imme-
ate family. It is not long, however, before it is introduced to the
tle box in the corner. The box that can create magic. This box
n take you on journeys to far-off places only once dreamed of.
nimals that were once only seen by the privileged few now
habit your front room. *Mickey Mouse*, *Power Rangers* and
undreds of other children's favourites dance out of the screen.
oung minds marvel at the colours and sound that come out of it.
he box has begun to weave its spell.

ounds familiar

ime to go to bed Jane', shouts the mother to her 9-year-old
aughter. Ten minutes pass and the only sound that comes from
e living room is that of the television. Jane is lost deep in the
rogramme. 'Jane', shouts her mother once again, 'It's getting
te. If you don't go to bed, you'll be tired in the morning.' This
me there is a reply from the front room, 'Five more minutes';
en by way of an afterthought, 'please'. Another ten minutes pass.
his time the mother storms into the front room and says, 'You
ways push your luck too far, Jane. To bed now.' As the television
switched off Jane storms up the stairs. 'It's not fair,' she yells, 'all
y friends are allowed to stay up until ten o'clock. I hate you,
[um.' With that the bedroom door slams shut. The battle has
egun.

John is eleven going on sixteen. Both his parents work so he has
s own key to the front door. After school he lets himself into an
npty, lonely house. He throws his bag in the corner, grabs the

crisps and Coke left by his parents to keep him going until the
get back at 6.00p.m. He sits down in front of the TV and switche
the video on. His friend has given him a pirate copy of *Bas*
Instinct. An ice-pick in the brain as the man reaches sexual clima
oral sex and violent sex are shared with the crisps and Coke. Th
battle is raging.

Dan is twelve and very excited as he goes off to his friend, Paul
for his party. Dan's parents are happy for him to go as they kno
Paul's parents well. Ten other teenagers are invited to the party.
starts with a meal at Burger King followed by a game of ten-pi
bowling. Afterwards they make their way back to the house for
video. Paul's parents consider themselves broad-minded and a
not perturbed that he has chosen a '15' rated film. Dan watche
both horrified but strangely enjoying what he sees. The battle
out of control.

Wendy is a single mother who has done well to bring up h
three children on state support. Tim is fourteen, Rob eleven ar
Joy seven. Tim and Rob share a bedroom while Joy has to slee
with her mother. Life is hard; the children are a constant battle. 7
help give herself a bit of peace she bought Tim and Rob a telev
sion set for the bedroom. What they watch, she doesn't know ar
has no energy left to care. The system has seen to that. Sometim
when she goes to the toilet in the early hours of the morning, sh
can see the glow from the television under the door. The batt
goes on.

Great invention

Television is a great invention. It can bring into your room imag
not even dreamed of. It can be used to inform nations of event
Who was not moved by all the images from around the world
communism collapsed? It is a great medium. What parent has n
sighed with relief when 3.30p.m. arrives and you know that the
is an hour of good entertainment on television. Your son is capt
vated for one whole hour! It frees you to get on with other jobs
simply collapse next to him! What parent is not grateful for t
video when your child is at home, sick and bored.

The role television plays in our modern culture was captured b b DeMoss who rewrote the 23rd Psalm:

> TV is my shepherd, I shall not want.
> It alloweth me to lie down in my reclining chair.
> It leadeth me beside Luke and Laura.
> It entertaineth my soul.
> It leadeth me through many a dull afternoon – for the
>   advertisers' sake
> Yea, though I walk through the valley of the shadow of
>   boredom, I will fear no evil.
> For thou, TV, art with me.
> They game shows and soap operas, they comfort me.
> Thou preparest a daily programme schedule before
>   me, in the presence of my TV guide.
> Thou anointest my head with a sea of sensuality;
>   my discretion runneth out.
> Surely good times and mindlessness will follow me
>   (and *All My Children*) all of the *Days of our Lives*,
> And we will dwell in the presence of thy *Guiding Light*
>   forever![24]

The problem starts when television becomes a substitute for
parental involvement. Television becomes a problem when there is
o control over what is watched. Censorship is a very difficult area.
ost would agree that extremes are wrong – sex with children is
ne example. The difficulty arises with other greyer areas. For
xample, *Cracker* with Robbie Coltraine is a very well produced
rogramme. It has tackled many sensitive areas including rape.
ome of the rape scenes shown were very disturbing. Were they
lid because they were raising a real issue? Did they encourage
pe? Should some of the scenes have been cut? The debate will go
n, for what is acceptable to one is insulting to another.

What is clear, however, is that parents can have some control
ver their children. All the examples at the beginning of the
napter are understandable. I understand why parents allow it to
appen – I do not blame them. It is hard – it is a battle. But for the
ke of our children we must fight it. Up to a certain age we can
ntrol what they watch. Whatever the rights and wrongs of

censoring films, parents can and should monitor and control what their children watch. The blame does not lie totally with the producers of the programme. Certainly we should campaign against some of the standards that programmes promote. Equally though we have a responsibility to censor what our children watch. I appreciate that the child will reach an age when this is no longer an option and we will look at that later. However, the standard should have already been set.

CHAPTER 8
'Turn that music down!'

John smiles as the house is finally empty. His parents are at work and his brother has just gone over to his mate's house. John goes into his bedroom, takes out the latest Oasis CD and puts it in the player. He turns the volume up so that it will shake the very foundations of the house. He stands in front of the long mirror, crumples his hair, and waits. The music hits the first note and the voice of Liam Gallagher rings throughout the building. The music now transports John from his bedroom into Wembley Stadium. He now is Oasis and all the fans are screaming at him. He jumps about in front of the mirror, playing an imaginary guitar, and singing into a comb, trying to remember all the moves his hero made. If his mother were to walk in now, she would find her son singing with all his heart. He would be embarrassed; she would be amused. He is just one of millions who have done the same thing.

Many of us have been on the same journey where we are transported from our bedroom to some national concert hall. We have been Elvis, The Beatles, The Rolling Stones, Marvin Gaye, Led Zeppelin, The Police, The Jam, The Housemartins, The Cranberries and Oasis. The music may have changed, but its power is undiminished in every generation.

The centrality of music to modern lives cannot be overestimated. Twenty-four hours of MTV videos, Walkmans and CD players are all part of the air young people breathe. There are very few shops you can visit where music is not playing. More and more shops have televisions hanging from the ceiling pumping out song after song on video. Even hairdressers and dentists have got in on the act with music videos playing. Music is everywhere you go.

It may all be new to us. But it's not to young people. It's what

39

they've grown up with. They know no different. And that's the point – it is part of their culture. They are not afraid of it. Some adults may be, but they are not. I can't stress this point too much. Music is as much part of their lives as breathing is. When we look at the subject i.e. music, we need to be very aware of that fact. It does not excuse the excesses, as we shall see, but it means that we must try to understand it.

Music, a source of conflict

The problem with music and young people is that it often becomes a point of conflict. The choice of music and the loudness of it can become points of tension in a family. This should not really surprise us because there always has been, and will be, a generation gap in music. When I was young my parents described The Rolling Stones as not being real musicians; their music was far too loud, and finely it was all a waste of time as they could not make out any of the words they were singing. Today I find that I do not like rap or dance music. I tell teenagers that it's not real music, it is far too loud and I can't make the words out! As I express those views I begin to smile because I realize that I'm saying exactly the same things my parents said to me a few years ago.

In other words a musical style can really be understood only by the generation that it came out of. That's not to say we cannot appreciate or even like it. But the point is that it is music of the generation. The older generation will never fully understand a new generation's music. The reason I do not really like rap and dance is primarily because it is the music of a different generation. That's not to say that I can't appreciate it; nevertheless it will always be slightly alien to me.

It is very important that we understand this when we look at modern music. All too often adults will make value judgements about rap and dance based on style as opposed to content. We must not make judgements based on taste. Because I do not like a certain style of music, does not mean that it is wrong. The issue of the right and wrong of music is to do with the lyrical content and the context.

As parents you may find some of your children's musical taste puzzling. You will be making a big mistake though if you judge whether it's appropriate for them to listen to by your distaste for it. Just because you find it too loud is not a good reason for banning it.

Music is a gift from God and a central theme in the Bible. It was used to soothe a tormented soul (1 Samuel 16:15–17). Music was used to celebrate a victory over an enemy (Exodus 15:19–21). Music was used to thank God for His justice (Psalm 9). The Bible is full of references to music. One Psalm is full of exhortations to praise God with many different instruments (Psalm 150).

It is a lovely gift that we are meant to enjoy. I appreciate that some people have justifiable concerns about pop and rock music which I deal with in the next chapter. However, the fact that there are abuses does not mean that all music is intrinsically wrong. Some of the lyrics in opera are very unhealthy, but I do not hear anybody claiming that all opera is wrong. No, we recognize that all God-given gifts can be and have been corrupted.

Before looking at some of the abuses of music in the rock and pop world, I should like to look at some of the positive aspects of this gift.

Reflecting the soul of life

Music is often a reflection of people's ongoing pain and frustration. As an example, parts of Handel's *Messiah* were written as he was going through great personal trauma. He was locked up in prison for not paying his debts. Despite his circumstances he continued to write and towards the end he had a vision of angels ascending and descending into Christ's presence. He wrote the 'Hallelujah Chorus' as a sign of hope in dark times.

Beethoven became stone deaf. This is reflected in his music into which he poured more and more of himself as he desperately fought against the encroaching disability.

Modern examples that music is often a reflection of people's ongoing pain and frustration are numerous. Phil Collins on his first two solo albums is pouring out his emotions over his failed marriage. One of Sting's albums was written after the death of his father and captures the emotion of that experience. Bruce Springsteen's *Tunnel of Love* album was written after his marriage failed. He also wrote the very moving 'Oscar' winning song, *Philadelphia*, which deals with the trauma of AIDS. U2 write many songs about the pain of life. *I Still Haven't Found What I'm Looking For*, is an honest reflection on their spiritual journey. Genesis wrote about the despair of being homeless. Peter Gabriel and Kate Bush sang about the dehumanizing effect of unemployment. Some of the best rap music deals with racism and other injustices.

In other words music is a reflection of the soul. If you want to know where a culture is, music is a good place to start as it is often beating with the soul of the nation. Music is written by people who experience life, and their lyrics often reflect that. Take as an example Mary Chapin Carpenter who wrote a song called, *Joe Doe No. 24*. Why did she write a song with that title? She wrote it after seeing a headline in *The New York Times*, 'Unknown Since 1945, John Doe No. 24 Takes His Secret To The Grave'. The story was about someone who was deaf, mute and blind and who was found wandering the streets of Jacksonville, Illinois, in his teens. His identity was never established. There were no missing person reports. No parents came forward to claim him. He had no name. They called him what they did simply because he was the twenty-fourth unidentified male in the state psychiatric hospital. In explaining why she wrote the song, she said:

> It's not so much a metaphor for existential loneliness as
> *it's about the fear of being lost and forgotten.*

In that song title she has captured the heart of our modern culture. That's what music can do because music is a reflection of the heart.

Take another group: Soul Asylum. One line from their hit song, *Homesick*, says:

> I am homesick for the home I never had.

Those lyrics reflect the *angst* over the broken, dysfunctional families that many of our young generation come from. The lyrics are expressing the reality of modern life. The reality is that more and more young people are coming from broken homes. The truth is that more and more of them are looking for a real sense of community, a real sense of belonging. That is the world in which young people live and that music often reflects.

Marc Cohn is an American singer and songwriter who deals with many life issues on his album, *The Rainy Season*. One deals with the ongoing struggle to live — to get through each day. The chorus echoes many a person's wish:

> One day/There's love for the lonely/One day/ they will walk in the sun/One day/Rest for the weary/Rest for the weary ones.

The Beautiful South write songs about life in modern Britain. Again they capture some of the anguish of modern life. One of their hit singles, *A Little Time*, was about the breakdown of a relationship. It was sung as a duet with a man and woman. The chorus was sung by the man and the verse by the woman.

> (Man) I need a little time to think it over/I need a little space just on my own/I need a little time to find my freedom/I need a little . . .

> (Woman) Funny how quick the milk turns sour/Isn't it, Isn't it/Your face has been looking like that for hours/Hasn't it, hasn't it/Promises, promises turn to dust/Wedding bells just turn to rust/Trust into mistrust.

Trust into mistrust. Is that not life? Is not that the way relationships begin to break down? See, some of these musicians are tackling the big issues of life. They are writing about everyday events.

Sometimes music can capture the core of our spiritual being. It can capture the heart of our quest. In 1982 Bruce Springsteen released a very stark album, *Nebraska*. In it he deals with man's need to be reconciled to God. I don't know if he believes in God, but he deals with the issue in the song, *My Father's House*. In it he is dreaming that the Devil is chasing him. He runs to his father's house for protection. But when he gets there he discovers that the house is empty and his father is not there. The song finishes with the following lyrics:

> My father's house shines hard and bright/It stands like a beacon calling me in the night/Calling and calling so cold and alone/Shining 'cross this dark highway where our sins lie unatoned.

Bruce Springsteen is just reflecting what many artists have done over the years, a yearning for more than this world apparently offers.

I start with the positive because I want you to realize that the music scene is not all bad. The way some people talk you would think there was nothing good in it. That is patently not true. Beneath the sometimes tacky, even destructive elements of the music world there is often a longing for something spiritual. Music is often an honest attempt to interpret the times. When it works, it's great.

Role models

I shall never forget one day when I stood in a newsagent's. Next to me was a mother with her 9-year-old daughter. All that the daughter wanted was the magazine about Kylie Minogue. To the girl Kylie Minogue was a goddess. The young girl was not unusual. Thousands of teenagers have posters of East 17 or Take That adorning their walls. That is normal; young people look for role models – heroes to follow. Very often these will be pop artists.

What we need to realize is that the 'teen artists' may appear to be targeted at teenagers. But in reality they are marketed at 9 to 12-year-olds. Bands like Wham, Kylie Minogue, Bros. and Take That. They become the child's heroes and they 'buy' into the image. They copy what they wear, how they walk and talk. And you have to ask: what role models are they for these young people to follow? Are they setting an example which we are happy for children to follow?

Musicians are uncomfortable with the idea that they are role models. They would argue that all they do is to play music. I wish it was the case. But the reality is that young people need heroes and role models. That's why youngsters buy any magazine on Take That. That's why what Bono says is important to many.

I don't have much sympathy for musicians who say they don't believe that they should be role models. It strikes me as inconsistent to knock a system or a person through a song, but then not to give a positive alternative. Simply Red wrote a song, *Wonderland*, which attacks the politics of the Thatcher years. It is a powerful song demonstrating the power of music to be a social commentator. If musicians use lyrics in that manner, then they too must be accountable. The standards that are used to judge others will in turn be used to judge you. That seems very reasonable to me.

Music is powerful because of the power of the artist over his audience. I think we would be foolish to dismiss it.

CHAPTER 9
As nasty as it really gets

We have seen that music is part of our teenagers' lives. But we also need to recognize that it's very big business. In itself that is not bad except when our children are exploited and their moral values bombarded simply in an effort to increase sales. We are talking about a multi-billion pound industry that has increasing power. Corporations like Sony are buying up more and more of the market. To describe the size of this business let me give two examples from the lives of two 'superstars' – Madonna and The Rolling Stones.

How big is 'big' business?

Madonna arrived in New York City in 1976 with $35 in her pocket. By 1994 she had sold 85 million albums worldwide. She is reputed to have a personal fortune of over $70 million. Time Warner gave her a contract that was estimated to be worth $60 million. Pepsi paid her $5 million for making one advert. Phil Collins, Michael Jackson, Sting and George Michael are just a few of the others who are in the same wealth bracket. Below them are other major acts who are treading the same path.

The statistics of the 1994 Rolling Stones world tour are staggering:

- On average, it took 200 plus road crew members four days to assemble the stage.
- A fleet of fifty-six semi-trailers, nine custom-fitted buses and a specially refitted Boeing 727 was used to move The Stones and crew around.
- They used nearly 4 million watts of generated power

produced by 6,000 horsepower generators. That's enough power to run a town of 25,000 people.
- Their staging used 170 tons of steel and aluminium. According to a press release that is, 'enough steel to build 180 white Ford Broncos and enough aluminium to manufacture 275,000 cans of Budweiser'.
- The production budget for each concert ran between £500,000 and £750,000.
- In terms of sound, The Stones used a system powered by 1.5 million watts – that is roughly as loud as 10,000 home stereos cranked to full volume.

Music, then, is big business; it is part of our lives and for the record companies their number one objective is profit. We are fooling ourselves if we think that the company is more interested in the art form – it is not. This means many things, but as far as this book is concerned it has one vital consequence. Controversy is very good publicity which brings sales. If you do not believe that to be true, let me give you an example from the advertising world. Benetton have used a series of highly controversial posters in their recent campaigns. But that was the heart of the strategy – create more publicity and therefore sell more product.

So an artist who 'trashes' his hotel room, is caught in possession of drugs, has many girl/boyfriends and is foul-mouthed is good for sales. To write lyrics that get banned is good for business. The music industry thrives on excesses.

As an example, some would argue that Madonna is a very shrewd businesswoman. The reason she courts controversy is for one reason only – to sell more records. The sexual image that she presents is not in the cause of women's liberation, as some argue, rather it is simply to sell more records. Who knows? I suspect that not even she does anymore.

So remember who really is exploiting your children with some of the music. It is easy to blame the artist, but I would also suggest that behind him or her is a much bigger force.

There is no doubt that it is big business and unfortunately for our teenagers there is no bigger business than sex and the focus on physical pleasure as an end in itself. Seldom do young people entertain the notion that a human being might be more than a collection of body parts and hormones. Life is nothing more than an endless series of conquests and seductions, occasionally interrupted by naked rage at the opposite sex.

Many adults are puzzled about what to do. They wonder about the problem of censorship and freedom of speech. They want to protect their children, but at the same time they don't want to be over-protective.

What we need to realize is that our modern culture is so different. Whereas in the past Elvis may have gyrated a hip, today's heroes simulate the very act of sexual intercourse on stage. In the past The Beatles had thousands screaming at them; today bands take fans on to the stage to join in some of the sexual games. The world of rock and pop today is a far different proposition from the past. Children have constant access to music through the radio and CDs but also through personal Walkmans. Who has not sat on a bus or a train and heard the muted sounds coming from somebody's earphones as they listen to the latest rap? The message of music is pumped into children's minds all the time. And, of course, there is now the development of CD roms and the potential explosion of sound and visual images.

What, then, are some of the things that are going on?

The heart of the problem

In 1994 Janet Jackson toured America. She is a very polished performer with a very visual show. To make sure that the thousands in the auditorium don't miss it, five video screens are mounted around the stage. This way the audience can watch every small move. During the concert she sings her hit single, *Any Time, Any Place*. As she sings it she pulls a young man out of the audience. He is made to straddle a chair. With 100,000 people watching, with close-ups provided on the video screens, she begins to massage his crotch. The sexual game is allowed to go on for a while before security guards lead him off.

In 1987 Guns n' Roses album, *Appetite for Destruction*, sold over twelve million copies. They are one of the world's top bands. One of their songs had these words:

> Panties round your knees, with your ass in debris . . ./Tied up,
> tied down, up against the wall.

This was followed in 1991 by *Use Your Illusion II* which had a song
on it, *Pretty Tied Up*. This described a woman as a 'bitch' who
desperately wanted to be whipped and abused by all the group.
The song had these lyrics:

> She ain't satisfied without some pain/Friday night is goin' up
> inside her – again.

And it is not only women who are denigrated by Guns n' Roses.
Take the song, *One in a Million*:

> Police and niggers, that's right, get outta my way./Don't need
> to buy none of your gold chains today . . ./Immigrants and
> faggots, they make no sense to me./They come to our
> country and think they'll do as they please,/Like start some
> mini-Iran, or spread some f****** disease.

Is it really any wonder that we are creating generations that have
no respect for authority? Do we wonder why racism is still a major
problem in this country?

2 Live Crew, a rap group from Miami, had the dubious distinc-
tion of having their album, *As Nasty As You Wanna Be*, declared
obscene and banned by state law. This may have happened in
America, but they are big in our country. Titles of songs on the
album give an indication of their possible content. *Bad Ass Bitch*
and *Me So Horny* are but two that one could mention. Bob DeMoss
of Focus on the Family analysed the album. In fewer than sixty
minutes of sound, he counted 226 uses of the f*** word, 163 uses
of the word 'bitch', 87 descriptions of oral sex and 117 explicit
terms for male and female genitalia.

Prince, who no longer calls himself that, wants to be known by a
symbol because he sees himself as neither male nor female. His
song *Gett Off* has the following lyrics:

> Everybody grab a body, pump it like u want somebody . . . Gett
> Off – 23 positions in a one-night stand.

Let me now just list some other artists with their lyrics and make no comment. Perhaps these are bands that your children listen to:

Y?N-Vee. Song Title: *4 Play*

> Kiss me baby right there/you know what it does for me. Sweet ecstasy . . ./Just give me wine and you can have all of me/Massage me all over down to my vee . . .

TLC. Song Title: *Red Light Special*

> I'll let you touch it if you like to go down/I'll let you go further if you take the southern route/Don't go too fast, don't go too slow/You got to let your body flow.

Salt-N-Peppa from the album *Very Necessary*. Song Title: *Shoop*

> Slip slid to it swiftly/felt it in my hips, so I dipped back to my bag of tricks, then flipped for a tip, made me wanna do tricks on him, lick him like a lollipop should be licked.

Snoop Doggy Dogg from the album *Doggystyle* (sold more than 3 million copies). Song Title: *G Funk Intro*

> We travel in packs and we do it from the back, how else can you get to the booty? We do it doggy style – all the while we do it doggy style. He f***** the fleas off the bitch; she shakes the ticks of his d***, and in her booty he buries his mother******* bone.

Eazy-E from the album *Eazy-Duz-it*. Song Title: *Still Talking*

> Tell ye mama to get off my tip, I have no time to give her my d***. I'm gonna hold it and walk around the stage and if you f*** up I'm gonna get my gauge and unload the barrel and laugh 'cause I'm puttin' lead in your mother******* ass. Psychopathic, but the hos (whores) are attracted because when I'm all hard my d*** is at least a yard. In the days of old when I was a nut, now I need at least three hos when I f***.

Nobody will ever convince me that lyrics like this will not dehumanize a person. You can't pump that into somebody's mind without it affecting his or her value system. The lyrics treat humans with less dignity than a dog.

Is it any wonder, then, that every day we read in our newspapers about more rapes and violent attacks on women? Could there be any connection between such violence and the lyrics? How do we expect our teenagers to behave if what they listen to encourages them to treat humans like animals? What has our country come to when under the much abused banner of freedom of speech it allows lyrics like that into young minds?

It is the sign of a country that no longer has a meaning. It is the sign of a country that has lost direction as regards moral values.

CHAPTER 10
False images

The media, through films, advertising, magazines and soaps presents untrue images. Take just four areas that are fundamental to who we are, body image, sexuality, sex and love.

1. Body image

I remember a famous singer and actress explaining how she kept trim, beautiful and young-looking. She put it down to plastic surgery, the right diet and a daily three-hour work-out with her personal trainer. I wonder how many young girls have looked at her and wished they could be like her. How many teenage lives have been hurt because there is no way they can match her? Who can afford a special diet, and even if cosmetic surgery is justified, who can afford it? Who has the time or the money to work out for three hours a day? But there is a more subtle image at work. The inference is that this person is the norm. The image is created that we should all strive to look like her. Success, so the image would have us believe, is looking like her. It's an image that is sold to us as truth.

At the 1991 Psychologists Conference Dr Andrew Hill reported that one in four girls were worried about their body shape by the age of nine. Dr Hill was very concerned about the trend:

> At best we are conferring on some a lifetime of discontent with their physical appearance and eating behaviour. At worst, there is the potential for an explosion in clinical eating problems.

Dr Hill said that children were absorbing the same cultural pressures as adults. Role models on television and in fashion articles emphasized slimness.

Recently *The Sunday Times* looked at the whole question of image and made this observation:

> A report appeared in the *British Medical Journal* posing a fascinating question: if the shapes used to model women's fashions were projected on to real, flesh and blood women, what effect would it have on their health? In the 1920s, the *BMJ* pointed out, mannequins were pear-shaped, with ample hips, narrow chest and broad thighs, conforming fairly closely to the average healthy female form. Since the 1960s, though, a terrible thinning has taken place and the most extreme vital statistics were found in the case of . . . Barbie. If the world's best-selling doll were made flesh, she would be so far below her natural body weight that she would suffer from irregular or non-existent periods, reduced sex drive and infertility. To sustain her slimness she would have to starve herself. In short she would be anorexic.[25]

Health clubs are booming, diet books fill our bookshops and personal trainers are popular. Why? Partly because we are more concerned with health. The main reason, however, has to be because we are trying to develop the so-called 'perfect' body. Millions are spent on trying to get the image. Because that's what it is – an image. The tragedy is many young people buy into it. They feel of little value because they do not have the body.

Who can blame them when they are bombarded from all quarters? Magazines that flaunt the 'perfect' body, TV presenters and actors are all cut from the same mould.

Ask yourself a question as a parent or concerned adult. What message do I convey about body image? What 'tattoos' am I leaving on young people's minds? There is nothing wrong with dieting. The problem is when it becomes a social institution. Everybody knows you diet; you tell everybody how much weight you've lost this week. Your conversation is diet-centred. There is nothing wrong with dressing smartly. The problem is when it becomes an issue. You are constantly buying new clothes.

If you make these minor issues major events in your life, young people will pick up the message. They too will learn that we measure worth and value from the clothes we own and the body we possess.

2. Sexual stereotyping

If body image is one issue that is affected by the media, another is that of sexual stereotypes. Sexual stereotyping is labelling certain human characteristics as male and female. For example it is acceptable for women to cry in public, but men are considered 'wimps' if they do. Men are allowed to be career-minded while women are meant to sit at home and cook the meals. Sexual stereotyping says it's a woman's job to do the washing-up, hoovering and ironing. It's the man's job to do the gardening, painting and car mechanics. A lot of the media show the men doing these jobs; roles are often reversed and this becomes a selling point. That is sexual stereotyping.

A few months ago I went with my wife to buy new units for the kitchen. The salesperson approached us and directed all his questions about cooking towards my wife. He naturally assumed that because it was the kitchen then the woman was in charge. Not only is that sexual stereotyping, it is bad salesmanship!

When you turn to television and advertising in particular you would expect them to be breaking down these barriers. But apart from some notable exceptions the majority of adverts reinforce the idea that the woman does the washing, the man the painting, the woman the ironing and the man cuts the lawn.

3. Sex

The third issue that the media distorts is typified by films such as *Pretty Woman* and *Four Weddings and a Funeral*, by soaps such as *Neighbours*, *Eastenders* and *Coronation Street*, and by some magazines. The overriding emphasis is that if you feel like it, do it. We are created to be attracted to members of the opposite sex. That is normal and healthy. If you find yourself attracted to somebody that is great. But our culture, and in particular the media, have taken it a step further by twisting what is good and saying every time you feel those things its not only normal, but you must satisfy them. You both have the feelings, you've got the opportunity in the back of the car, your parents' house, your mate's house or wherever – do it! The culture and the media simply say that it can happen in any place you want – all that matters is that it happens – it does not matter if it's destructive as in the film *Dangerous Liaisons*; it does not matter if it's violent as in *Fatal Attraction* or warped as in *Blue Velvet*. The key is that it happened. And they create this image that says that every time it will be wonderful.

Showing it like it is?

How many of you have seen a TV programme or a film where the act of sexual intercourse was a disaster? In films it's always silk sheets and romantic music. If it's a PG rated film you will see a couple go into the bedroom, the lights go out and the sequence fades. If the director is artistic he might show a train going into a tunnel or smoke come out of a chimney. If it's a '15' rated film you will see half-naked people and a lot of groaning. With an '18' it's the full works – nothing is left to the imagination. But one thing is common to all films – the sex is almost always wonderful.

Take a recent film, *Pretty Woman* with Richard Gere and Julia Roberts. It is a 'feel good' factor film in that at the end you feel good about life. The storyline is that Richard Gere, a wealthy business man, picks up Julia Roberts, a prostitute. They return to his penthouse apartment at the hotel where she asks to be paid. He pays her and then she pulls out four condoms and says, 'I've got a green one, a blue one, a yellow one; I'm out of purple, but I do have a gold condom, the condom of champions – nothing gets through this sucker!'

There are two things to say about that sequence. But first a general comment about condoms. Millions of married people use them and are generally happy with the way they work. When discussing the use of condoms with young people that is not really the point. We need to be aware of what the issues really are in this whole area. However, the film is a good example of the way false images are created about condoms. Julia Roberts says that she has a gold condom; nothing will get through this sucker. That is a lie. No condom is 100 per cent safe. The BSI (British Standards Institute) will accept a failure of 2 in 100. Durex report that the failure rate of condoms is between 7 per cent and 15 per cent. Second, in America it is known that a certain percentage of prostitutes carry the HIV virus. The issue is not addressed in the film. All that happens is that they have sex.

Robin Hood, with Kevin Costner, was a film which was targeted at young people. It was a good film apart from one or two points. It trivialized and to an extent glorified rape. In the closing scene the Sheriff of Nottingham tries to rape Maid Marian. The scene is made out to be very funny and I distinctly remember all the audience in the cinema laughing. That disturbed me as rape is a terrible crime. He does not succeed because Robin Hood rescues her, but to my mind the damage has already been done to our minds.

Four Weddings and a Funeral has a scene where the two central characters recount how many sexual partners they've each had. One is not at all embarrassed to admit to over thirty. There is no issue of love or relationships; in fact it's made out to be a bit of a joke.

The above films are not considered controversial like *Natural Born Killers*, *Thelma and Louise* and *Basic Instinct*. *Pretty Woman*, *Four Weddings and a Funeral* and *Robin Hood* are the average modern films that whisper their distortion of truths into our ears. That is what is disturbing and frightening.

Magazines

One does have to question the wisdom of some of the content of teenage magazines. *Mizz* magazine, aimed at 14 to 18-year-olds, ran a summer special on sex. There was advice on every conceivable aspect of sex, and a few more besides. Do our children really need to know about bondage, troilism and masochism? One editor of a teenage magazine explained their policy with these words:

> Most of our readers are aged 14 to 16 and a lot of them have had sex once. They want us to write about real-life issues, like

the pressures they are under from their peers . . . And most of all, they want to know how to do what they want to do or feel they ought to do to please boys. They want the sort of sophisticated technical information they're not likely to get from parents and teachers. (My italics)

I suppose that by that argument if they wanted to make a nuclear bomb we ought to print the instructions! By that argument whatever people want – you give it to them. There is no question about moral frameworks, or how sex can be damaging. It really is only fun and a part of growing up. I wonder why we have a crisis?

A lot of the emphasis is on risk-free sex – 'oral sex', 'anal sex', 'ten ways to please your lover', 'how to have an affair', 'does size really matter?' and so on. It is all part of the image factory.

4. Love

The trouble with the media is that they confuse romantic with real love. And if they confuse the two the chances are that we will follow. Romantic love is the sensation we have already described – the sweaty hands and the shaking legs. Romantic love gets you all in a dither, but oh – it feels good! The person you like walks into the room and there is a real physical sensation. There is a drifting mooniness in thought and behaviour, the mad belief that all your dreams have rolled themselves up into your beloved, a conviction that no one on earth has ever felt so overwhelmingly about a fellow creature before. They are great feelings and the really good news is that psychologists tell us that we shall have five of these experiences in our lifetime. The bad news is that the feelings last for only three months. So enjoy them while they last!

Romantic love is very real, the emotions are strong and in every sense we believe that when it happens to us, it's the real thing. No amount of talk by friends will change that view. This, for you, is the 'real thing'. You will travel to the far corners of the earth for your loved one. For some it may develop into real love. For many, they are left bewildered and hurt.

It was probably captured at its best in one of the hit films of

1993, *Sleepless in Seattle*. The core of the story is two people, Annie and Sam, who do not even meet until the end of the film. They are separated by thousands of miles, but fate has dictated that they are just meant to be together. She is a career woman and he a widower with a marvellous son who is convinced that his dad will never fall in love again. The whole tone of the film is best captured by the statement:

> What if someone you never met, someone you never saw, someone you never knew, was the only someone for you?

Though separated by thousands of miles she hears his voice on a radio phone-in and destiny finally brings them together.

Now the whole point of the film is that it is pure Hollywood fantasy. That is one of the strengths of films – they occasionally help us escape the harsh realities of life. What is frightening is that millions upon millions will buy into the romantic notion of the film.

Take a modern teenager who goes to the average school where success is measured by one of three standards – academic, sporting and the arts. She has no interest in the arts or sport and although not dull, she does not excel academically. She will leave school with a couple of certificates and no prospects. She is now locked into a cycle – how does she and a million others get out? Some turn to crime, others to drugs for the thrills and escapism, others just die inside and become another statistic on the local doctor's list. Others, however, for a brief moment catch the advertisers' dream:

> What if someone you never met, someone you never saw, someone you never knew, was the only one for you?

And they believe it because everything they read and everything they watch tells them it's true. But above all they will believe it because like all of us they want to be loved. They have bought the lie that romantic love can fill the deep dungeon in their life. And for a brief moment it happens; they will discover the 'perfect' him at the local night club. There is magic in the air. Life seems worth living. He is the answer to her deepest desire. In the magic of it all they have sex and contrary to all expectations it's a disappointment. He obviously lied; it was his first time and he was uncertain what to do. It's messy, hurtful and embarrassing. Nine months later she is just another statistic in some bureaucrat's speech. But she is real, she has feelings, emotions and she is slowly, emotionally dying.

Romantic love is a great thing and we want to encourage people to enjoy it. But we must guard against making it the foundation for a lasting relationship. Too many lives have been broken by its false promise.

Teenagers need to be taught that these feelings are normal and that they can enjoy them. They do not need to be lectured on the morality of their feelings or for how little time they will last. Rather we need to laugh with them as they go on and on about their new partner. We smile as they yell at us that we never will understand how they feel. We hold them tightly as they sob because the dream has ended and they are beginning to learn about the lie. We all want to be loved; don't sell our young people short with a substitute for it.

three
The result of the seduction

It came as something of a surprise to discover how easily and effectively you can be destroyed by getting what you want.
Joel Reading

We expect our two-week vacation to be romantic, exotic, cheap and effortless. We expect anything and everything. We expect the contradictory and the impossible. We expect compact cars which are spacious, luxurious cars which are economical. We expect to be rich and charitable, powerful and merciful, active and reflective, kind and competitive. We expect to eat and stay thin. Never have a people been more the masters of their environment. Yet never has a people expected so much more that the world could offer.[26]
Daniel Boorstin

When I look at society and think of the millions of children exposed every day to its toxicity, I am in near despair. My despair comes not only from the progressive loss of spiritual and idealistic values, but from the fact that our present society is not working.[27] *Dr Benjamin Spock*

CHAPTER 11

Echoes of confusion –
the world of young people

. Young people no longer know what truth is

was an average classroom with an ordinary group of teenagers
at could have been in any school in Britain. I was there, at the
vitation of the teacher, leading a class on the subject of values.
Ve discussed a number of issues including the difference between
right and a wrong action. How can we know if some actions are
ght and others wrong? The group was silent. I tried to help them
long by giving an example. 'Robbery', I explained, 'is a wrong
ction.' Suddenly one of the boys came to life – I shall never forget
hat he said.

> 'Robbery is not wrong,' he said; 'it's only wrong if you get
> caught!'

Tragically he was serious; this was not some joke – the right or
rong of robbery was not in the act, but in being caught. If you
ould steal something and get away with it – well done. It was a
hilling moment because it made me realize how far we have
noved as a country in our value system. It's a sad day when our
ense of right and wrong is not judged by the act itself but by the
esult.

Recently I was involved in a radio discussion on the subject of
ex and marriage. The others involved included a lady from Relate,
eenagers from a local youth club and a couple of students from the
ocal university Christian Union. The discussion started and I put
orward the view that sex was best enjoyed within the framework
f a lifelong relationship. The teenagers from the youth club

disagreed and we got into some healthy discussion. Then, and much to my surprise, the students from the university Christian Union said they did not agree with me either. This surprised me because these were Christians who were sincere in their belief about living out their faith. I challenged them by asking how they could justify that position when the Bible clearly states that sex is reserved for marriage. The answer was a classic:

> The advice about sex was good for the time it was written because they didn't have condoms so God gave those laws to protect us! But now we have condoms it does not apply anymore.

Their logic was classic. The Bible was written around 2,000 years ago. At that time there were no condoms available and therefore the only safe sex was with one person for life. So when God gave His commandment that sex was to be experienced only in marriage it was for health reasons. God gave the commandment to protect us from disease. Today, however, we have contraception and so the law is outdated. Now that we have condoms, there is no risk and so we don't need the law about sex and marriage!

The absurdity of the argument was lost on them. The fact is that condoms do not make sex safe – they reduce the risk, but they do not make it 100 per cent safe. But even more absurd is the thought that God's advice is somehow lost in a time vacuum. When God gives advice He is aware of what is going to take place in the future! God's law about sex was not primarily given for health reasons, though that is a consideration. God gave them because the moral framework is a good one.

In another school I had a discussion with a group of students about many subjects; politics, the environment, Jesus, sex and so on! At one point I simply said, 'What we need to understand is that values must be based on truth.'

As quick as a flash the students came back to me, 'What is truth?' and 'What makes you think that you have a line on truth?'

This is our modern culture. This is the world teenagers live in. It's a culture that is tolerant and holds all views to be equal, and that no set of values is better than another. But it is equally intolerant of anybody who might claim some standards to be universally true. In other words there is no longer one system of beliefs that is absolute. There is no one standard by which we can measure behaviour and decide what is acceptable.

There is no better example of this than one from the music world. It is reflected in singers such as Prince. Prince is the same and yet different from the black singers from the 50s through to the 80s who were raised in a narrow legalistic form of the Christian faith. People like Little Richard, Marvin Gaye and Al Green. They all have tried to come to terms with the sexuality of their music and their life in contrast with their upbringing. And frankly it has driven them mad. Because they were brought up with one set of truths and then they began to live out another set, but could not rid themselves of the past. They found it incredibly hard to choose between two gods. For Prince there is no such problem – you can hold both truth, although they be opposite. So it is possible for him to simulate sexual intercourse, oral sex and masturbation on stage, but also to sing songs about salvation and the cross. He sees no problem with this. He is the perfect example of our modern culture.

In the past our society turned to the standards of the Judaeo-Christian faith for help. Not everybody held that faith or believed it was true, nevertheless the central morality of the faith was recognized as the foundation for our country. Although the change apparently took place in the 1960s – the seeds for the change had been there for many years. The increasing knowledge of science, two world wars, the work of Freud, the writings of the 'new' authors such as Lawrence, Scott Fitzgerald, Hemingway all changed prevailing standards. The cumulative effect of this was reflected, first in major changes that Parliament made to the law. Second, it was also shown in so-called 'flower power'. This was a movement of free sex, cheap drugs and music. It was more than just people having so-called fun. There was something new. They were not just violating accepted standards of behaviour – they were saying there are no accepted standards of behaviour. The idea seemed good and has stayed with us. Though the flower power people of the 60s are now in their forties and fifties they have brought their world view with them – there is no accepted

65

standard of behaviour. That's not saying that they don't have any standards – they do. Rather it means that there is no universally accepted standard.

The decades of the 80s and 90s are very different from the era that most of us grew up in. Today's culture is radically different which is one of the main reasons why we find it so hard to understand young people. They live in a different world that lives by different standards. That is why it is so hard for parents – so don't despair, you are not alone!

2. Young people have no identity

The second consequence of living in the modern culture was highlighted by a conversation I had with a teenager in our youth club. I thought that I would show them that I was in touch with the youth scene. So I commented that they must belong to the 'alternative' set. With great indignation and a look which said what do you know, they replied, 'Certainly not, we're grunge'. A few months later I bumped into them again and casually asked how the grunge crowd was getting on. Again with indignation they said they were no longer grunge and were now . . . frankly I can't remember and I've given up trying to follow all the changes and shifts.

As my encounter in the youth club shows this change is reflected in teenage culture. Up until the mid-80s most young people identified with two or three groupings. Groupings such as mods and rockers, rock and soul, punk and soul, and so on. But since the early to mid-80s there has been an incredible explosion of different groups – grunge, goths, rave, dance, jungle, and so on and even within each category there are subdivisions. There is fragmentation of youth culture. In fact it is almost becoming that not to be part of a group is the in thing – although if enough people do that it will constitute a group!

The result of all this is that all these groups have different codes of conduct, different clothes, different standards and different values. Then society fragments – it breaks down into smaller and smaller units.

This fragmentation has a number of consequences, but the most devastating must surely be that each group has its own view on truth and standards. Other groups can hold truths, but they have no bearing or relevance to your group. This is dynamite. First it makes debate difficult if not impossible because groups have different codes of reference. Secondly, parents, teachers, youth workers are a very different group from the teenage cultures. This simply means that teenagers will have codes of belief which are often at variance with their parents. To discuss an issue with them is, therefore, very difficult because they are happy for both 'truths' to be held in tension. So while they can see that one group believes drug taking is wrong, the group they are committed to says that it's OK. They are happy for both truths to stand side by side. This is the pick and mix culture. You can pick and choose what suits you at any given time. Furthermore you can take different beliefs and mix them together.

An interesting but disturbing result of this pick and mix philosophy was highlighted by another classroom discussion. We were looking at suffering in the world and in particular at the war in Bosnia. I could not get a word out of them – there was a kind of glazed look on their faces. Somehow I mentioned animals and with that a young girl came to life. 'It's terrible,' she said, 'dogs are really suffering and nobody is doing anything.' Please understand that I believe that animals rights are a very important issue. It is right that people speak and campaign on behalf of animals. But what disturbed me that day was the fact that human suffering could not get a reaction, but that of animals did. It is a clear result of the pick and mix culture that sees all issues of equal value and you respond to the one that you think is important. There is no value system – humans, animals and vegetation; they are all of equal worth.

Young people no longer have a reason for living

Perhaps one of the saddest results of all this is that it has left young people feeling hopeless and helpless. One of my great complaints about young people today is that they are so apathetic. Gone are the days of protest and passion. Today if a politician or church leader falls, young people are not shocked – they expect it. This element of despair was highlighted by the tragic death of Kurt Cobain. Kurt Cobain was the lead singer of Nirvana and in 1994 he shot himself to death. He was a very unhappy man which many put down to his parents' separation when he was eight. He wrote songs such as *I Hate Myself and Want to Die* which were probably a combination of two things. I'm sure the song partly came out of depression but it was also a reflection of his views of the hopelessness of life. The music of Nirvana represents a generation that sees no hope for the future.

In this country those views are expressed by groups such as the Manic Street Preachers and Radio Head. The Preachers' last album *The Holy Bible* is a brilliant, bleak masterpiece that captures the heart of a generation that has lost its way. The lead singer with this group is Richey James, a depressive and a self-mutilator. At the time of writing he has been missing for over two months after leaving his car near the Severn Bridge. It is a very sad story, but what is even more moving is that it struck a chord with tens of thousands of teenagers. It seems that what he was trying to write and sing about has captured the hearts of many young people. With his disappearance, in one sense, went their last hope. His disappearance prompted a long correspondence in *Melody Maker*. Typical is this letter from a girl:

> I wish someone would wake me up and tell me that this has all been a nightmare. But it's real, and I wish it wasn't.

The response in *Melody Maker* has been so overwhelming that they printed an article on the Samaritans with helpline numbers (a good example of responsible journalism).

As a reflection of this despair, the teenage suicide rate has increased by 71 per cent in the last ten years. Commenting on this disturbing trend, Jeanie Milligan, psychotherapist in the adolescent department of the Tavistock Clinic, London, said:

> The capacity to feel nihilistic and to fall in love with death is quite common at a superficial level in adolescence. But the rise in young male suicides suggests something beyond normal adolescent gloom.

Perhaps the mood of the moment is captured by Radio Head and their album *The Bends:*

> I'm just . . . waiting for something to happen, and I wish it was the Sixties. I wish I could be happy. I wish, I wish, I wish that something would happen.

There is a real sense of despair amongst the young. But why should we blame the young? After all it's our generation that has created the culture that has sucked any life out of them.

A generation that caused the problem

We no longer have dreams. We no longer have people who lead and inspire. We are a generation that is dull and cynical. We do not help someone if they are mugged in front of us. We are the generation that has created the high divorce rate. The result is that young people are careful about commitment as their experience of it is summarized in one word – pain. Corrupt politicians are thought to be normal. We reward the rich at the expense of the poor. We seem to glorify a National Lottery whose founding principle is gambling. We have created a climate of insecurity in regard to jobs. There no longer is such a thing as a 'job for life'. Commenting on this problem Ms Milligan said:

> Adolescents tend to take security at home for granted, and they are considerably shaken if either of their parents get made redundant. They end up confused in a very particular way, worrying about their parents when it should be the other way round.

We have created the loan generation mentality. More and more students are getting into large debt. We no longer respect the law. The environment is in crisis – who, amongst adults, cares? The world moves from one disaster to another but we feel impotent to do anything. Is it any wonder that the cartoon characters Beavis' and Butthead's cynical, irreverent, and nihilistic views of the world are so appealing to the young?

The Church is often no better. A week does not seem to pass

without some story of a church leader having an affair. There are rumours of misuse of money. As one young person said:

> I used to want to be a super Christian. The reason I stopped pursuing that goal was because I had no role models. All the people from my church are hypocrites.

And we wonder why the young are generally apathetic. Just take a look at the role models! They are only reflecting you and me. Teenagers will deny it, but they do follow our examples. And the tragedy is that we have taken them down a dead-end street. How can we expect teenagers to react positively in such an atmosphere?

I believe that all this has left our children open to the two major influences of modern culture.

1. Materialism

It's four weeks to Christmas and today is the day you buy the presents for the family. You head off into town tired, weary and snappy and it's only 9 o'clock in the morning! But you feel like that for one simple reason. Primarily it is not because of the hassle of parking, or the difficulties of finding a table for a mid-morning coffee, or the number of times people tread on your toes. No, the reason you feel this way is because you are worrying about what presents to buy people. What do you buy your wife, your parents, auntie and uncle? It's a big problem affecting all of us every Christmas. Do you know why? Because they already have everything. We worry about what to buy them because they've got everything and we just don't know what else they would want.

That is the stupidity of our culture – it persuades us to buy something we don't need. You have a video player, but not the latest one. The latest one not only can play videos, but it can sing, make the tea and recite the complete works of Shakespeare! If we do not purchase this new video our life will be incomplete. Of course, purchase it and there will be yet another video player that you just have to buy.

This is the heart of Western philosophy – to give people the maximum choice of consumer goods. Western society is founded on the principle of people buying more and more goods. It has to do that to survive. The whole of Western governments' strategy is based on the principle that people will buy more and more. If we don't, our countries will become bankrupt. To that end the West's way of life is apparently not only the most desirable in the world, but appears to most people to be the only viable one.

As we saw in an earlier chapter the main vehicle for maintaining this view is advertising. It is its role to sell us things we don't need. This is done by convincing us that the new product will meet a perceived need. But all it does is create a tension. It is a tension for those who do not have, for it leads to a perception that having these goods will fill some deep need. It is a tension for those who have listened to the dream and bought all the 'goodies' only to discover there is still a great hole in their lives.

As a result we have created a value structure which is based on materialism. Success is measured by the amount of possessions a person has. Survey after survey in the 80s painted a picture of teenagers whose main ambition was to have a well paid job and a nice house. There is nothing wrong with a good job and nice house, but it's the motivation for having them that is in question. To want them simply because they allow you to buy more and more goods strikes me as being a shaky foundation for life.

Michael Jordan is considered to be the greatest basketball player ever. He recently retired and this is what *The Guardian* newspaper had to say about him:

Schoolchildren recently surveyed in China agreed that the two greatest men in history were Chou En Lai and Michael Jordan. In Britain where National Basketball can be seen only on satellite television, Jordan was the first choice of Brighton students when asked by Gallup which of sixteen celebrities most influenced their values. And *Playboy* declared last year that Jordan was 'more popular than Jesus', to borrow a phrase from John Lennon.

Jordan's astounding popularity led some sportsmen, notably tennis's Arthur Ashe, to wonder about the less healthy aspects of sports celebrity. Here was a whole generation of black youngsters, it was argued, growing up bombarded by the image of Air Jordan, desperately poor kids whose only desire was to own the latest pair of $100 Nikes – even if it meant mugging somebody for them – and whose only ambition was to play pro ball.[28]

Michael Jordan earned around £2.6 million in salary but made a reported £23 million in endorsements from Nike, McDonalds, Wheaties, Quaker Oats and Sara Lee.

While not justifying youth crime, are we surprised that robbery is a major problem in our country? If we constantly bombard our children with the value that success is measured in terms of materialism they may try to achieve it by many methods. First, they will commit their whole lives to acquiring more and more possessions by working harder and longer. Second, if they are unable to find work they will take those goods by the only other method available – stealing them. Third, why work hard if they can enjoy the same benefits by stealing them? Fourth, they work but still want the goods they can't afford – so they steal them. They justify this by the simple logic that they have been told that it's our right to have these things.

2. The 'me' mentality

I sometimes go to a leisure centre for a swim. On one occasion when I was changing, I observed another man who was ready to go and do his body building. He wore all the right 'label' gear from his trainers to the sweat-band. However, what really amazed me about this man was that before he went into the gym he checked himself in the mirror. He brushed his hair, tucked his shirt in, checked the socks were turned at the right place – generally he was making sure he looked 'good'. I could not believe that a man who was about to work out would be so concerned about how he looked. But for me he was modern man in a nutshell – obsessed with self. If one word describes our modern generation it is – me. The me mentality.

The 1992 general election was predicted to be a triumph for the Labour Party. After thirteen years in government the Conservatives were going to be beaten. The polls predicted it and the experts confirmed it. However, as we all now know, the Conservatives retained power. I recall a television debate analysing hat had gone wrong for the Labour Party. The mistake, the analysts said, was to have made one of the central policies of the ampaign a tax increase. It was the threat of a tax increase that rove the voters back to the Conservative Party. I will not forget a mment made by one of the experts:

> It just confirms what I've believed for a number of years; we have become a more self-centred and selfish society.

his attitude has its roots back in the 70s with the influential aching of psychologists like Carl Rogers. It was he who xpressed the view that it is my undeniable right to realize my full otential as a human being – in my sexual practices, in my ambi- ons, in my health and in every other way. Of course, if I am to alize my full potential, then my neighbour takes second places. he result? We have become a very self-centred culture.

Nothing sums this up better for me than a recent television rogramme. It was a television special to present an award to a ck-singing legend for an outstanding contribution to music. here is no doubt that he deserved the honour as he has one of the lassic' voices of British rock and pop. At the end of the presenta- on he made a speech. The heart of the speech was his looking ack over his life and realizing that there were three goals at the art. Number one was to be in a job for longer than six months, umber two was to save £500 to buy a sports car, and number hree was to 'pull as many birds as possible'. He proudly nnounced that he had achieved all three. What values does such a atement communicate to young people? Is it any wonder that we ave a teenage crisis with such role models?

he result

Jow we can understand why the teenager thought that stealing as only wrong if you got caught. In his culture stealing was not rong and it only became an issue if you got caught. Even then the sue was not just being caught. Rather it was the fact he had failed his task and the group he belonged to would know about it. hat is why it was wrong – he would lose face with his group.

The Christian students were only living out the philosophy of the time when they said that sex before marriage was all right. It felt good, it didn't do any harm and the Bible was right only on the issues with which you agreed. They were consistent.

That is why the other students were indignant that I dared to claim that there were some truths that must be universally accepted. Not any longer. A truth is held only if it benefits me.

Has all this change made for a better quality of life? That's obviously impossible to measure. But what I do know is this. As we saw, the teenage suicide rate, drug taking among teenagers, teenage crime and anorexia nervosa are all increasing. This year a new book, *Psychological Disorders Among Young People*, highlights the nature of the problem. The number of young people suffering from depression has doubled, if not trebled, since the war. The book points out that one (of many) factors that may cause this problem is parental divorce. This is a response not only to the separation of parents, but also to the marital discord that inevitably precedes it.

The statistics highlight that all is not well and point to the fact that there is a great deal of confusion, pain, hurt and isolation amongst young people. The causes of this are complex, but a lack of accepted standards of behaviour is one major contributing factor. Teenagers do not need more freedom – they need clearer boundaries. Boundaries give them security. They may say they don't like boundaries but they do give them security.

Please don't despair, for there is hope. As one who believes in God I should of all people have hope. For He is the God who gives hope. We need to be a people who start to give a lead again. We need to take a few risks and dream a few dreams. We need to become role models who offer hope. We need to start fighting back!

PART TWO
Fighting Back –
Creating a Foundation for Life

In the midst of this onslaught is there any hope? People simply feel overwhelmed by it all. They just do not know where to begin. I believe that the Bible offers us God's wisdom. That is why time and time again I quote from it. There is hope, but it will take hard work on your part. The heart of the Christian faith is hope in a God who transcends cultures and barriers. So by God's grace I do believe that it is possible.

There are four weapons which I believe are vital in our armour, if we are to give our children the chance of avoiding . . . *The Seduction*.

CHAPTER 12

Weapon one
The battle for the heart – unconditional love

The media scream at our children: if you look like this, do this – if you are winners we shall love you. But we must fight back with a greater weapon – unconditional love. If there is one quality that is greater than any other in the development of a life it is unconditional love. Unconditional love accepts your teenagers for what they are. It is the guiding light for bringing up your children. Without it your parenting will be very confused.

Unconditional love accepts your children despite the hair style or the clothes they wear or the things they do. You may not like the style – in fact I would be surprised if you did! But you still love them. Unconditional love rides with them through the ups and downs of the teenage years. It does not depend on exam or sporting results. They may get straight As in their exams – you're delighted and you love them. They may fail all their exams – you're disappointed, but you still love them.

Do you love me?

The most important question a teenager wants answering is – do you love me? Nothing counts more than that question. If they know that you love them, it will give them the emotional strength to cope with all the difficulties that life brings.

One observation I can make is: take me into any room that has two teenagers or 2,000 and give me a bit of time with them. After a while you can generally spot those who come from homes where they are shown unconditional love. It's not that they are brighter, better dressed or better looking. No, there is something about their personality, something about the way that they hold them-

selves that lets you know 'we feel secure'. It's not that they
arrogant, just a deep knowledge that they are loved.

Many teenagers are loved but it's conditional love – and th
know it. Conditional love is based on performance. The teena
observes that more warmth and love is shown towards them wh
they achieve certain things – good marks at exams, a position
the rugby team, another grade in music exams. They have lear
that they are valued not for who they are but what they ha
achieved. Most parents would be horrified to think it's the v
they operate – but sadly it often is. Life has taught us that edu
tion is important, which it is. But increasingly in the last 15 to
years it has become the answer to all problems. So teenagers
put under enormous pressure to pass exams and go on to hig
education. There is nothing wrong in that in itself, but it is wr
when the demonstration of love is based on the results. Certai
with most parents it's not deliberate, but teenagers will pick
the small signals that you give about this. Encourage them in th
studies, support them in their musical and sporting achieveme
but love them for who they are – not what they achieve.

How do they know you love them? It's because you tell th
and you demonstrate it. The two must go hand in hand. You
tell teenagers that you love them, but if the actions do not dem
strate that truth they will just see straight through it. You nee
be consistent in this.

Communication

My wife and I have occasional heated discussions! They can
about a number of things but usually the bottom line is tha
don't talk to her. Or sometimes I talk but I'm not communicati
As a church leader, I have sat in many church meetings where
criticism is levelled that we do not communicate. The lack
communication is often at the centre of many breakdowns. Tha
because we are social beings who function at our best when ther
interaction between us.

The Bible is a book which gives advice on many practi
subjects, one of them being the issue of talking to teenagers. T
is what the book of Deuteronomy says:

> These commandments that I give you today are to be upon
> your hearts. Impress them on your children. Talk about them
> when you sit at home and when you walk along the road, when
> you lie down and when you get up.   *6:6–7*

That was written over 3,000 years ago yet the truth is just as relevant today as it was then. And I think the most important point it
makes is that it is a way of life. This issue of talking to your children is not something that you just type into the diary, it is an
issue of lifestyle.

To communicate with teenagers you need to give them three
things: time, attention and positive affirmation.

Time

From the earlier chapters you will know that the average person,
including teenagers, watches three hours of television a day. It has
been shown that the average father spends three minutes a day
talking with his children. Those statistics really tell us where our
children get their values from. The values that television pours
into our living rooms are having more impact on our children than
anything else is. The way to effect change is down to one thing –
time. We need to spend more than just three minutes a day talking
with our children. This is of fundamental importance, as expressed
in the song *The Living Years* by Mike and the Mechanics:

> Every generation blames the one before and all of their
> frustrations come beating on your door. I know that I'm a
> prisoner to all my father held so dear. I know that I'm a
> hostage to all his hopes and fears. I just wish I could have
> told him in the living years.
>
> Crumpled bits of paper filled with imperfect thoughts. Stilted
> conversations, I'm afraid that's all we've got. You say you just
> don't see it, he says it's perfect sense. You just can't get
> agreement in this present tense. We all talk a different
> language, talking in defence. Say it loud, say it clear. You can
> listen as you hear.

A song written by a son after his father had died, expressing his regret that they'd not learned how to talk. The song is moving because we recognize the truth:

'I wish I could have told him in the living years.'

The point is ever so simple. It begins the day your child arrives, by your communicating love and warmth. Communicating truth to them. The brides you build in those early years will stay for the rest of your lives. The way you do that is by spending time with them. There is no substitute for it. You may think that money will buy you the time – it won't. You may not think that if you just work a little bit harder for a little bit longer, then you will have the time – the day will not come.

It may be that you have teenagers to whom for one reason or another you did not give time in their early years. I do not want to give you a guilt trip or a sense of having no hope. The good news of the Christian faith is that there is always hope – so hang in there. I is not going to be easy and it may be painful, but there is a way for you to start building those bridges. It will begin with an act of humility on your part because you need to sit your children down and apologize and ask for their forgiveness. And we are never too old to do this. If you think that you have failed your children in this area, talk to them – no matter what your age. Explain to them why you did not have time – be honest. But then you need to ask them to forgive you and to give you the chance to start again. Now that is hard, but as far as I know it is the only way to get there.

Focused attention

I had been working with young people for four years when suddenly realized that I couldn't go on any longer. I don't mean that I wanted to give up youth work, but rather that I was emotionally washed out. My batteries were on empty and if I did not do something soon then I would be in serious trouble. remember walking down our main street with tears streaming down my face. I called in to see one of my best friends who happened to be a doctor, and he told me that I needed to take some time off. To do this I had to see one of the leaders of the church worked for. It was a Tuesday lunchtime and he was a senior partner a very busy law firm. I knew that his diary would be full and I would have to wait a few days to see him. Nevertheless my friend insisted that I drop into his office and try to see him. I shall never forget the day because he came straight out of his office and told his secretary that he was taking me out and that he did not know when he would be back. I was overwhelmed by the man's concern and love, but above all by the fact that he gave me time when I needed it.

And that is exactly what teenagers often want, time when you can least afford to give it. But that is what you must give if they are to know unconditional love. Some of it will be spontaneous, but in truth much of it will need to be planned. The planned part is where you have a regular weekly event with your children. It may be that you take them to a football or rugby match; you may take them swimming or it could be that you go to a local coffee shop and spend half an hour with them. The important thing is that it's time which is theirs and it says that you care for them.

I am not suggesting that deep meaningful discussions will take place, but you will be building bridges for that to happen one day. Teenagers can be sullen as they go through a transitional period and their communication is often in single grunts. Don't force them to talk. Don't lose your temper and yell something like, 'I'm giving you all this time; you could at least talk to me!' It will not do any good. It just confirms to the teenager that you resent spending time with them. Hang in there because a point will come when the grunts will change to a few well chosen questions. The few questions will soon develop into their sharing events with you that have happened in their day.

When they do begin to talk, listen and take an interest in what they say. The more you are prepared to listen to their view, the better the chance that they will want to hear your point of view.

Positive affirmation

This is short and simple – tell them daily that you love them. Put your arm around them, give them hugs and tell them that they are special. Speak positive words into their life. Reinforce good behaviour. Be proud of your children in public and always speak

positively about them. All of us, but especially young people, ha
incredibly low self-esteem. I can't stress enough the vital role
parent plays in building up a child's self-esteem. If you are forev
putting your children down, they will build a defensive wa
around themselves which you will not be able to break dow
Don't say things such as, 'That's really stupid! Next time thi
before you open your mouth', or 'Do you know what your proble
is – you're lazy. In fact if you don't get your act together you w
achieve nothing in life.' Or 'What are you wearing? Can't you f
once make an effort and look decent?'

Be honest and think about yourself. Which comment stays
the memory – the positive or the negative? It's usually the neg
tive, which demonstrates its destructive power.

As you talk with your children be honest about your past. Ta
about some of your failings, but use them positively. This is n
meant to be a blackmailing session. Honesty is one of the brid,
builders in dealing with people.

Action Points

- **Praise your child at least once a day.**
- **Give your child at least one hug a day.**
- **Take time every day to sit and talk with your children.**
- **Never run your child down in public.**
- **Ask their opinion about something.**
- **Be honest about your failures.**
- **Have a laugh with them.**
- ***Tell them you love them – daily.***

CHAPTER 13

Weapon two
The battle for the mind – teaching your children to be critical thinkers

The point will come, and probably already has when your children will want to watch TV programmes that you feel are not beneficial to them. This is always a point of conflict! How can one tackle the problem? As with all things to do with young people the problem started when they were much younger and they observed, probably unknown to you, what you watched. In other words if you think that certain programmes are unhelpful to your child you need to have set an example of your showing restraint.

If your life is dominated by television and you spend hours in front of it, you may have problems setting standards with your children. If you constantly hire out '18'-rated videos and try to censor what your child watches, do not be surprised if you encounter resistance.

You need to set certain boundaries early on. When they are young, go through the children's schedule and agree with them what they can watch and what they can't. Furthermore, the amount of time they spend watching television as well as its content is an issue here. Then, and this is very important, you have to explain to them why they cannot watch certain programmes. Tell them what you think is wrong with the TV content. In other words you are not censoring in a vacuum; rather you are explaining why the content is unsatisfactory. In doing this you are helping them to develop a critical mind. It is a mind that questions what it watches; a mind that can differentiate between good and bad.

Consider where the television is placed. Does it dominate the room and are all the chairs facing it or is it kept in one corner? In many cases the layout of the room is governed by the position of the TV. If our seating plan is governed by the television it dictates to us our priority – watching television. If this is the case – change the layout. Have seats facing one another. Place the television in a place which does not dominate the room. Now when you sit in the room you are not automatically looking at the television, but at one another. It may seem a small thing but it really is a major change. If you do this over a period of time your priorities will change.

I believe that a television in a child's room is unhelpful for three reasons. First, it is a lot of temptation for a child to resist. It is hard enough for us as adults to control what we watch. It is asking a lot of a child to have the same restraint. Second, you have no control over what they watch. Of course, this may mean that you take yours out of the bedroom to set a good example. Third, and perhaps most importantly, it encourages isolation. The young person will spend more and more time in their room watching the TV which makes it more difficult for you to spend time with them.

Finally you need to be creative. Have the occasional family video night. As a family you get in a pizza and you watch a good video together. This will show that you are not against videos or television. In fact you are for it when there are good things to watch. It also means that you are in control and can choose what you watch.

As the children grow you can begin to watch programmes with them and ask what they think of the content. Ask them what values the programme portrays and whether they are healthy. In other words begin to create in your child a mind that is able to recognize what is good and bad and right and wrong.

Censorship is partly about banning things, but it should be more than that. We need to create positive alternatives for teenagers. We need to help them develop critical minds that recognize what is good and bad. That starts with you and me setting the standards.

As I keep saying, the greatest role model for young people is you! The extent to which television becomes a part of their lives is initially dictated by the attitude you as a parent show towards it. It is often hard to be objective in these matters, but I have suggested three steps that will help monitor what and why you watch television. Hopefully if you try these out, it will help you to discover the tattoos you are leaving on your child's mind by your attitude to television:

1 Over a manageable period, i.e. a week or two, check how much television you watch. For this to work you need to be honest! Record what you watch and note whether you deliberately watched it or whether you simply sat there because you had nothing better to do. How much do you use the video? What do you watch on it? Hired films, recordings or a combination of both?

2 Pick a number of programmes ranging from children's television to programmes shown after 9.00p.m. Monitor how they represent the family and singleness. What attitudes to violence and sex do they convey? Are you happy with what you see? Do you ever censor what you watch?

3 Try living without the television for a week. See what difference it makes to your life. What different things did you do? Does it make things more difficult or easier?

Help them to think for themselves

As I have already said, we need to teach our teenagers to be critical thinkers. They need to be taught not to accept everything they read or watch. Again this process begins when they are young. But as they grow you will want them to learn a number of things about our culture.

First, they need to understand the world they live in. Talk to them about the forces that mould our thinking. Teach them what is behind advertising – the truth and the lies. Give them the skills to accumulate all the facts and make informed decisions. Let me remind, of the big lies that our children face. They need to recognize these for what they are – images that hide the truth.

1 **Materialism** The most important thing in life is owning possessions.
2 **Relativism** Truth is relative to the group you belong to.
3 **Meism** It is my right to be fulfilled in all areas of my life.

Help them to understand that we cannot live in isolation. We are part of a community and we have a major contribution to make towards it.

Secondly, help them understand the difference between right and wrong. So few people today have any concept of the difference which is probably one of the most worrying aspects about our culture. Teach your child what is right and wrong. Teach them that certain kinds of behaviour are not acceptable.

Finally, encourage them to make rational decisions. Help them to learn the value of debate – to listen to both sides of a discussion. When they have all the information they can make informed decisions.

You may like to try a game with your child that will help them to become critical thinkers.

Spot the Lie

This is a game created by the writer Os Guinness to play with his son. Christopher was five years old and his father wanted to help him recognize the messages behind the adverts. The rules are simple: parents say, 'Spot the lie' when the advert comes on the television. The child has to pay attention and find the implicit lie or totally irrational statement in the advert.

It may be an advert which suggests that if you buy a certain perfume men will fall all over you. It may be that if you buy a certain cigar, peace will fall on your life; or it may be that drinking a certain lager will make you sexy.

In Os Guinness' case if his son spotted the lie, he was given twenty pence. Or you may have a game whereby when they spot ten lies you take them to the leisure centre, ten-pin bowling or any activity that they enjoy doing with the family.

This is more than a game. This will teach your children to have discernment in life.

Os Guinness was asked whether this could get expensive. 'Luckily for us,' he said, 'it worked the other way round. Before Christopher bankrupted me, he grew disillusioned with what he was seeing on television. He's eleven now, and he much prefers to read novels and do other things.'

Action Points

■ **The work starts when your children are young. At this age** you can have an agreed list of what they can watch.

- Keep videos and televisions out of the bedroom.
- If you are married, ensure that you and your husband agree that the children shouldn't see certain types of video, and then stick by your agreement. Your decision is what counts.
- Organize video nights so that as a family you sit down and watch one together.
- Always explain why they may or may not watch a programme.
- At the right age watch programmes with them and talk about the values they portray: how did the programme treat men and women? What did it say about sex?
- Plan a 'no TV night'. This means no television, Nintendo or Gameboys. Fill the evening with activities such as reading or playing some of those games that are gathering dust in the cupboard.
- TURN IT OFF! If you think a programme is unsuitable or if you feel that the child has been watching television for too long, switch it off. Don't be afraid to draw a line, particularly when peer pressure is pushing your child to see the latest blockbuster. Be ready with suggestions and be prepared to get involved with the child in doing something else.
- Be aware that they have access to friends' television and videos elsewhere. This is a very common and difficult problem with no easy answers. Try and find out what they watch. Ask the friends' parents. Children often want help when they do not want to watch them. The trouble is that once they are in somebody else's house they are out of control and the pressure to conform to the group is enormous. Talk to the children about it and suggest ways in which they can deal with the problem.

You can make a difference

A friend of mine was faced with exactly the sort of problem mentioned above. A few years ago his 10-year-old daughter, Julia, was invited to her friend's party. Her friend, Rachel, had decided that she wanted to go for a McDonald's and then see a video.

Rachel's parents agreed that they could watch *Dirty Dancing* as part of the party. This is a '15'-rated film. Obviously my friend was not happy about his daughter watching a '15'-rated video. First he watched the video with his wife and then he contacted the parents of another friend, Joy, to express his reservations about the video and to ask their advice. They too watched the video and decided that they would be unhappy for their 10-year-old daughter to watch it. My friend then sat down with Julia and explained that they were happy for her to go to the party, but not to watch the video. After a while Julia could see the logic of this. She then telephoned Rachel and told her that Joy and she would come to the party, but would not watch the video. Within a short period Rachel's parents telephoned my friend to say that there would not be a problem – they would not show the video. We have to be sensitive and at times firm, but we can make a difference.

Teaching children the positive side of music

The teenager sat down with his parents and began to moan about the music in the church. The words were outdated, the music was old-fashioned and it was boring. These were just some of the complaints which this young man mentioned. He was a Christian, but he just found it all a little bit dated. At first, his parents argued with him. This after all was their music and the words were great. Young people just did not appreciate good taste!

Does it sound familiar? I'm sure that it's a conversation that goes on all over the country after every church service. But this was 1690 and the young man was Isaac Watts! In the end, and I'm sure that it was to shut him up, his father challenged him to do better (often a good principle when people moan). And Isaac Watts did and he wrote over 350 hymns.

I start with that story because we need to realize that the controversy over music is not new. It is true of every generation. As I explained earlier, that should be expected since a music style is unique to each generation. But we do need to be aware of the problem. That is why in church circles, over the last twenty-five years, there has been a revolution in church music. One of the main pioneers of this is, of course, Graham Kendrick. And in a sense he has done what Isaac Watts did back in the seventeenth century. He has written songs for a modern culture.

That is not to say that you don't use any of the old songs. You do because some of them are clearly marvellous. But there does need to be a process where new songs are created. That has got to be healthy. So it is that new styles are beginning to emerge from 'youth churches'. We should encourage this.

Which leads me to my first point about music and young people. As with the media, so it is with music; you need to develop critical minds in these young people. Minds that can recognize good or bad music. The way you do that is by promoting what is good.

The trouble with many of us is that we are good at saying what is bad. It's much easier to be critical than constructive. But in the long term that is counter-productive. If you as a parent ban something, a record for example, or a video, you create a vacuum in your child's life. You need to fill that vacuum with something positive. If you do not fill it, they will. And further more they will resent you for it.

So promote what is good. That is why I started with the example from church. If your children find the church music boring, find them a positive alternative on tape. If your children come home raving about some new songs they heard at a Christian youth night – go out and buy the tape! The problem with many of us is that we try to defend what *we* like. And in that way we make a battle over something that should never happen. If your children find a Christian musical style they like, don't knock it. Don't say that you can't make the words out! Don't argue that it's pure emotion and the words are simplistic. Just buy it. Encourage them by being positive.

There are also many good Christian artists around: Eden Burning, Why, The Tribe, Martyn Joseph, to mention but a few British ones. From America there are Petra, The Altar Boys, The Choir, Doin and so on. There is a great range of musical style in that list. I'm sure that there is one that your children would listen to. Buy it for them. Help to fill their minds with positive images. There is a myth, however, that says that just because it's Christian music then it is good. This is patently not true. The tragedy is that some Christian music is very poor and some lyrics are also bad. You need to be an objective listener.

Of course, the question is asked, 'What principles do you apply to the music of artists who would claim no faith?' First, there is a section of music where it is very clear what is unsuitable and I gave examples in a previous chapter. It is very clear that the words of those songs are unhealthy.

As for the other music available the Bible teaches us to listen to what is true and proper. This, however, is a much more difficult area and Christians do have different opinions. But whatever choice is made, you need to explain the reason to your children. If you ban a child from buying certain records you need to give good reasons. You need to try and take them with you.

I try to apply three principles to musical lyrics. First, is the song a reflection of life? Second, is what they are singing about true? Third, does it bring dignity to humanity?

For example, a few years ago, George Michael sang, *I Want Your Sex*. Yes — it's a reflection of life. Yes — it's probably true. But does it bring dignity to humanity? No, it does not. Those lyrics depersonalize human beings and rob men and women of their self-respect. That's why I think Madonna is not suitable to listen to. Much of her music far from liberating humanity demeans its value and worth.

There are, however, many other groups who would fill all three criteria. Nevertheless care needs to be taken. I remember a couple of years ago I went to buy a friend's 16-year-old daughter a CD for a present. The band I picked filled all the above criteria, but as I read the lyrics there were a couple of matters I was not happy with. I chose not to buy it, but instead I got her another CD which I thought was acceptable.

If you are going to encourage your children in the positive it may mean a number of hours looking through the lyrics before the record is bought. Believe me it's worth it.

Action Points

- **Often children will try to tell you that they like the music only and that they don't listen to the lyrics. Do not accept that** excuse from your children. It's not possible to listen to music without taking in some of the words.

- Talk with your children about the lyrics. Explain why you don't like something. Give your reasons.
- Go to a concert with your teenager. This could be an experience for both of you!
- Encourage them with positive alternatives.

CHAPTER 14

Weapon three
The battle for the body – giving young people a clear sexual ethic

A question that often gets asked is this: when is the right time to tell my children about sex? The right time is from the day they are born! It is from that moment that your child senses and then observes your attitudes towards sex. This is expressed in the way you relate to one another. If as partners you do not hold hands or show demonstrable signs of affection, a clear message is given to your children. If you are embarrassed at home about nakedness, it communicates a negative message about the body. Sex education must begin by first demonstrating, then teaching, the power of loving relationships. Through our words and actions, we must familiarize our children with the vocabulary of relationships: love, honesty, intimacy, forgiveness and grace.

Positive Images

You need to be giving out healthy, positive images. Do not be embarrassed by the human body, but rather demonstrate a healthy attitude towards it. When the children are young, let them see you in the bath! This means that at a young age they will notice the biological differences and begin to ask questions. Don't avoid them! Obviously their minds will not grasp the major details, but they will have positive messages about the adult body.

Be demonstrative in front of them. Hold hands when you go for a walk. Kiss each other as you go to work. Again show that there is nothing to be embarrassed about. A major part of the battle in this area is one of attitude. Sex and sexuality are good gifts from God and we want that to be expressed to our children.

As they grow older the questions will get more detailed – don't avoid them. Tackle them by giving the information that will be helpful. In this way you are giving them the information little by little. This probably means that there will never be a time for the one-off talk about sex because you have taught them over the years. Even if that talk should take place, you will have laid a good foundation to build on. This is why it's important that from the day of birth a healthy attitude towards the body and sex has been developed. This means than when you begin to talk it will be a natural extension of all that's gone before.

For girls there is the big questions of periods. This can be a very disturbing time for girls. There are also many false things said about this subject in school playgrounds which lead to some girls developing a wrong understanding of the subject. That is why it is essential that you have talked the matter through with them before it begins to happen. Don't wait for the periods to start and then tell them; it must be before. Having said all that, you need to be aware that just because you have explained what is going to happen means that you can then forget about it. That is not true. For many girls even though they know what is going to happen, it is still a traumatic event. You just need to be there to help and support.

As your children develop into teenagers the questions and issues become more difficult. They want to know why you think sex is best enjoyed in marriage. To answer that needs more than, 'Because the Bible says so!' I hope that this book and the resources recommended will help you give a clearer answer.

A number of people, including some parents, think that it's the role of schools to give sex education. My experience is that schools provide a very good programme in sex education. They present all the views and cover all the issues. The content may vary from school to school, so be aware of what is taught. Ask the school to tell you – they are legally obliged to. That still does not make the school ultimately responsible for sex education. I strongly believe that this should come from the parents.

There are a number of reasons for this. First, you can teach them the values you consider to be most important. Second, all the surveys show that young people want to hear sex advice from their parents. Third, if you raise the issues, there is a much bigger chance that your children will discuss with you any problems they have. To help them you may want to give them a good book or tape on the subject. Give it to them to listen to on their own.

Don't believe that young people don't want to listen to their parents

One of the greatest lies around is that teenagers don't want advice from parents. Survey after survey shows that young people want to hear from their parents; they want your opinions on this and every subject. The 'Trust for the Study of Adolescence' found that:

> Without exception, young people wanted their parents to talk to them about sex.

They may not agree with what you say. That's what makes it so frustrating. Because your children want your opinions it's essential that you have some understanding of the issues. But above all they want to hear your views on sex and sexuality. So in the next section of the book we shall look at issues that teenagers want to know about, for example, masturbation, how far is one allowed to go in a relationship, and what is true love. These are the topics that young people always ask about. I cover them, not because I believe that there are any easy answers, but because I hope to help you enter a bit more into your children's minds. We are still in the heart of the battle for the body, but in the next few chapters I want to take you into the very minds of your teenagers.

Time and time again, as I meet with young people, the same questions come up. I have no doubt that if you were to talk to your children, they too would ask the same questions. In the hope that it might be of some help, the following section shows how I would tackle them. I do not claim that they are exhaustive answers or that you will agree with all that I say. You may wish to avoid some of them. But it's important that we tackle them as this is part of the battle and these are the questions your children are asking.

CHAPTER 15
The cost of love – it's just sex – what's the big deal?

I've observed a major image that young people believe in. It is this image that is causing so much damage. It is this image that is primarily responsible for all the statistics that I have quoted. The image? Put at its simplest: sexual intercourse – it's no big deal, it's a private act between two consenting people and has no consequences.

Certainly sexual intercourse should be and is a private act between two consenting people. This image, however, has developed because that is all that people think it is. The decision and the act may be private, but some of the consequences can have a much wider effect. The rest of this chapter looks at some of these tragic consequences.

Sexual intercourse is not a private act for four reasons:

1. Two people

Sexual intercourse is between two *people*. People have feelings and emotions. They can feel joy and pain; they can experience great love but also the pain of rejection; they can feel liberation but also shame. The way some people talk about sexual intercourse puts it on the same level as animals. Dogs do it, cats do it and even rats do it, so why not us? It treats people almost as lumps of meat to satisfy some basic desire. The act of sexual intercourse releases emotions that up until then none of us knew we had. To deal with these we need to be in a relationship that helps us come to terms with them. The number of people that have been hurt because someone has treated them like a lump of meat to be discarded the next morning is immeasurable. Sex is a precious gift that is not to be used lightly. It needs to be handled with great care.

2. Pregnancy

Sexual intercourse is not a private act because it has the potential to create the greatest gift of all – life. The action of two people coming together in sexual intercourse has the potential to create life and that is awesome. And for me this is one of the main issues. Life is the most treasured possession we have and yet we treat it so lightly. People have to be eighteen to vote; they have to take a test to drive a car; they have to pass some exams to get some jobs. But with life there is no problem; as soon as both partners are fertile, go for it! Anybody can have sex and have a baby. And it's crazy because the greatest responsibility in life is to bring up another human being.

In Hull, researchers found that most teenage mothers did not want children, but lacked the knowledge and assertion skills to prevent pregnancy. Dr Diana Birch, Director of Youth Support, a London-based charity that works with schoolgirl mothers, noted that girls will often try to deny to themselves that they are having sex. Furthermore, she said:

> Young people are often completely ignorant about sexual matters and do not fully appreciate the connection between sex and getting pregnant.[29]

The biggest risk is at the beginning: Birch says that 52 per cent of pregnant schoolgirls conceive with their first boyfriend. According to recent research there were almost 10,000 conceptions by girls under the age of sixteen, half of which were terminated. More than 4,500 girls under the age of fifteen become pregnant every year. It appears that those starting sexual intercourse before sixteen have a one in three chance of becoming pregnant before the age of twenty. And we are talking about life here; we are talking about a human being who is totally dependent on the mother and father. It's not a toy or some badge you wear; it's another human being.

Typical of teenage mothers is Tracy, who was fourteen when the first sexual pressure led to pregnancy. She had Laura when she was fifteen. After the birth she suffered a year of depression, partly because the father had gone with another girl, making her pregnant, too. Now sixteen, she lives with her baby in a home for young mothers. She loves Laura, a blonde toddler with an appetite for dancing to acid house music. But if she had her time again, she would not have a child so young.

> You've got the rest of your life to get pregnant. It's made me grow up really quickly . . . I feel like I'm an old woman. I feel about twenty-three.[30]

Here are some of the most fundamental issues all of us have to face, those of father- and motherhood. Are young people ready to take on the role? Do they realize the major change in life that a child brings? Is a 15-year-old boy ready to be a father? Sadly, there are men who when they discover that they've got a girl pregnant, distance themselves from her. There are a number of reasons for this, none of them justifiable. There is the fear of responsibility and the growing sense of being trapped. Men associate distance with lack of responsibility. So the less they see of the pregnant mother or the further away they move, the less they feel responsible.

My point is simple. The father may not spend one minute with the child, but he is the father. His lack of input into the child's life will have as big, if not bigger, an impact on his or her life as if he were around. Of course, if he is not around the impact will be negative.

That is why when we talk with young people about sex, it is not just about the act. It must cover the whole aspect of life, relationships, love, self-worth and parenthood because they need to see the act in its proper context.

What happens if your daughter comes home and tells you that she's pregnant? However hard, you have to realize that you can't reverse the circumstances by being harsh or unloving. Having a blazing row and shouting 'I told you so' would help nobody. Your daughter would need more understanding now than she has ever had. She would need you to be rational and to talk the issue through. She would need good advice. You might feel unable to give this. It might be that you would have to recommend that she talk to someone you trusted to give her good advice – a youth worker, teacher or counsellor. Above all you would need to love and support her through that time. (This issue is covered in more detail in Chapter 23).

3. Parents

Sexual intercourse is not a private act because it has the potential to affect others outside the relationship. The young couple who are having sex have guardians or parents who care for and love them. There are some teenagers, of course, who are not in that privileged position, and for them the issues are much more complicated. But the majority are cared for and loved. Sexual intercourse is not a private act because the consequences can affect guardians and parents. How many parents have sat listening to their son explaining that he has got a girl pregnant? How many have listened to their daughter explain that she is pregnant? I have seen the pain this has caused to parents. I have heard the questions they ask:

> Where did we go wrong? I thought he would never do anything like this. How could they do it after all we've done for them?

And the truth is that most parents haven't gone wrong. There are no simple answers, just a lot of pain. Often the greatest frustration is knowing that it could have been avoided. It's the pain of knowing the impact that this event will have on their young lives.

4. Sexually-transmitted diseases (STD)

Finally, sexual intercourse is not a private act because of sexually-transmitted diseases. An STD is caught from sexual intercourse and related activities. There is a great deal of ignorance about this subject on the part of teenagers and young people. This is worrying because it is a major problem in this country. Every year in the UK 500,000 people catch a sexually-transmitted disease.

In the UK in 1916 the only recognized venereal diseases were syphilis, gonorrhoea and chancroidal infection. By 1950 there were still only three recognized STDs. However, by 1960 there were sixteen recognized STDs and by 1980 there were thirty-two.

In America 33,000 people a day get an STD, that's 12 million cases a year. At that rate by the year 2000 it will be one in four people between the ages of fifteen and fifty-five. The message from America is a simple one: STD does not recognize a person's religious or moral belief, colour or creed, wealth or status – it recognizes only a person's actions.

Syphilis, gonorrhoea, genital herpes and pelvic inflammatory disease are some of the known STDs, yet it's AIDS and HIV that most people are aware of. As this is a subject that many parents want to know about, the next chapter will look at some of the issues.

CHAPTER 16

What's the truth about AIDS?

In the song to accompany the film of the same name, *Philadelphia*, Bruce Springsteen has managed to capture the pain that life brings to some people. In this case it is the devastation that AIDS can bring. *Philadelphia* is a very good film but it has two major weaknesses. First, it romanticizes homosexual relationships. I know of no homosexual relationship where the family is so universally accepting of the two men as they are in the film. Second, the film portrays death as a very romantic event. Death is never romantic.

Those two issues aside, it does a very good job of tackling a major social issue and presenting it to a wide audience. It shows homophobia to be a major issue in our culture. But probably more importantly it begins to deal with some of the major issues surrounding AIDS.

AIDS is the modern leprosy. In the past there was much fear surrounding leprosy. It was seen as the judgement of God and the people who had it were ostracized by the local community. There was very little understanding of it and from that ignorance sprang much prejudice, hatred and mistreatment. So it is today with the subject of AIDS. Some say that it is the judgement of God and those who have it should be cut off from their local community. Again there is very little understanding of the illness which leads to prejudice, hatred and mistreatment.

We do well to remember the Jesus of the Bible who demonstrated his great love for lepers. He talked with them but much more significantly He touched them and healed them. That was a clear indication of their value and worth. When we are dealing with those who have either contracted HIV or have AIDS, we do so as Jesus would – with love. It saddens me when I hear some of the language that people use when dealing with AIDS. We are talking about human beings who are very precious and greatly loved by God.

Some of the Issues

AIDS is short for Acquired Immune Deficiency Syndrome which results from contracting HIV (Human Immunodeficiency Virus). The first recorded cases were in America in 1981 and a year later in Great Britain.

AIDS differs in two ways from other sexually-transmitted diseases. First, one can be infected with HIV for up to twenty years without realizing it. Second, once HIV has developed into AIDS the patient faces certain death.

By April 1995 there were 1,864 known deaths from AIDS in Britain; there were a further 3,178 reported cases of AIDS and at least 30,000 people infected with HIV. According to the World Health Organization, by the year 2000 there will be 30–40 million people worldwide infected with HIV.

True lies

Despite all the information about HIV, people still have the wrong ideas about how the virus can be caught. It's not a gay disease although it seems to have started amongst homosexuals. HIV has increased more amongst heterosexuals.

The virus can be transmitted by a number of methods. Shared needles between drug addicts are a major problem in this country. It is possible for HIV to be spread by blood transfusion, but here the risk is now virtually nil. Children have caught the virus in the womb from their infected mothers. There is also evidence that under certain circumstances an infected mother can pass the virus on through breast feeding. Finally it can be transmitted in sexual intercourse.

Despite gossip and misinformation it cannot be passed by any of the following activities:

■ Hugging an infected person

- Sitting on a toilet seats which has been used by an infected person
- Swimming in a pool where a known HIV carrier swims
- Sitting next to an infected person
- Kissing an infected partner
- Being bitten by an insect

The judgement of God?

AIDS cannot be the direct judgement of God against immorality, as some have indicated. If this is true than a lot more people should be judged as well. For example, politicians who corrupt the truth, businessmen who exploit the poor, legislators who prejudice the immigrant – these are all people whom God says are immoral. Second, what of the innocent? the child born to an infected mother, the rape victim or the nurse who contracts the virus from a patient? If it is God's direct judgement then it is very indiscriminate and does not fit the picture of the God of the Bible.

STDS are among many graphic reminders that the human species is designed to function best according to certain standards. If we step outside those parameters, we begin to suffer painful results. This reality was brought devastatingly home to me as I watched *Philadelphia* at the cinema.

As I sat there with my friends, there was a special sort of silence in the cinema. The sort of silence that tells you something is happening between the film and the audience. It must be a magical moment if you're the director of the film, to sit there and realize that you have made it happen. The main characters have in some way stepped out of the screen and touched the lives of everyday people. There was a scene of a man in a hospital bed in America. He was dying from AIDS. His lover was with him as well as all his family. He had just won his court case and now he could die.

As the film ended, the lights went up in the cinema and many people were fighting back tears. As I walked out of the cinema there were clusters of people still in their seats, too upset to move. Some were moved by powerful acting that brought the issues to life. Others were stirred because they knew someone who had

ecently contracted HIV. But, I suspect, some were crying because
or the first time in their life it had dawned on them that actions
an and do have consequences – some of them devastating. For the
irst time they realized that the unprotected sex they had had with
ne or 100 partners meant that they were at risk. And maybe they
ried because they now knew that their actions could have put
hem at risk.

It is obvious that there are parameters within which the body
unctions best. All the medical evidence shows that the more
exual partners you have the greater the health risk. It's not that
he body is not designed for sex, just that it functions at its best
vith one partner.

Magic Johnson is a megastar of American basketball. A few
ears ago he announced that he had contracted HIV. It was a brave
nnouncement to make because people make strange value judge-
nents when they discover such things. One thing was certain; he
vould now discover who his true friends were – the ones who went
n loving him.

Magic Johnson was interviewed on the Oprah Winfrey show
nd asked what advice he would give to young people about sex.
his is what he said:

> I would advise all young people to talk to their parents. I would
> also say that abstinence (having no sex) or sticking with one
> partner for life is the answer.

hat is advice from a man who had many partners. He too can look
ack and see the mistakes and now he is trying to help others not
nake the same ones. He has realized that the human body func-
ions best with one or no partners.

The World Health Organization says that the only way you can
uarantee not catching HIV is to:

> Stick with one partner for life who you know has not got the
> virus, or abstain from sex.

All the evidence points to the fact that sex is best reserved for a
ifelong relationship. That is why it's essential that young people

are given all the information so that they can make informed choices. The freedom to say no to sex until one is in a lifelong relationship is not a puritanical, negative view. Rather it is the option that brings maximum freedom and the very best chance of a fulfilling sexual relationship.

CHAPTER 17

Why should I wait for sex until I'm married?

One question I always get asked is this: what is so special about sex that it should be kept for marriage? What we need to understand is that it's a good question! For those of us who are married, we sometimes forget what all the fuss is about. But we must never forget what it's like to be young. The thought of marriage is not even in the minds of young people. If it is to happen, it's way off in the future. I remember one teenager telling me that he was not going to get married for another twenty years. That would make him 36 or 37! Marriage is not the problem, rather it's that they have all this latent sexual energy and what are they going to do with it? The sex drive is most powerful in men at the age of eighteen to nineteen and in women in their mid- to late twenties. They have a lot of powerful feelings in their bodies. So we must take the question seriously, as we are asking them to put on hold what many of their friends consider to be normal. To help young people, we need to understand a number of things about sex.

1. Sex is more than just passion

It certainly is that! But there is more to it than pure passion. As I have said elsewhere, sex is designed so that we can experience intimacy. Intimacy is the most personal experience that you will have with another human being. In 1 Corinthians 6:16 St Paul talks about the uniqueness of sex in that when two people come together they in effect become one person. That's one of the reasons why penetration takes place in intercourse because it physically makes you one. But there is also something mystical about the union; something that locks the two bodies and spirits together.

There is a real sense of part of you remaining with that person. It
a part of you that you can never take back. To leave that perso
means that you have in essence left something of yourself wit
them.

2. Sex leaves you naked

I'm not talking about physical nakedness for it is possible to hav
sex without taking one's clothes off. Rather I'm talking abou
vulnerability. To have sex opens a side of you that few others see.
allows you to begin to discover a new dimension to yourself. W
are emotionally open before one another in a way that was n
possible before. In the act of sexual intercourse there are dimer
sions to ourselves that we were unaware of.

3. Sex is designed for its best use within marriage

I am not naïve in that I realize that many people have sex outsic
marriage and enjoy it. However, I would still maintain that th
maximum benefit and enjoyment of it comes when it's exper
enced within marriage which is the right context and place for se
It's to be in a lifelong, loving and trusting relationship. Son
think that this is a very restrictive view and that it makes Go
seem like a killjoy. The truth, however, is the opposite in that Go
has given instructions about sex and many other matters
liberate us. God wants us to enjoy life to the full and part of max
mizing that enjoyment is reserving sex for marriage. Far fro
denying human freedom these guidelines enable us to live to o
full potential.

CHAPTER 18
How far can I go in a relationship?

Whenever I get a group of young people together to talk about sex I can *guarantee* that one subject will be of no interest to them – marriage. There are two reasons for this. First, marriage is something they are not thinking about, let alone planning for. Second, their main interest has nothing to do with the rights and wrongs of marriage. Rather, their pressing concern is limited to how far they can go with their partner. If one is committed to not having sex before marriage, how far can one go? In a sense they have a list on which they want to tick off what is acceptable.

- Holding hands
- Cuddling
- Kissing
- Fondling breasts
- Fondling genitals
- Mutual masturbation
- Oral sex
- Sexual intercourse

These are big issues for young people and you need to have thought them through. Looking at the list I start with the last one, sexual intercourse, and search for principles. One major principle is related to your belief in God. This truth came home to me when I was eighteen.

At that time a committed Christian, I went to work at a major holiday camp. There you could get anything you wanted – drugs, sex, drink and so on. One night I took a girl back to the chalet; within one minute we were horizontal; within two minutes my

hands were going to places they should not be; within thr
minutes I was very close to going all the way and having sexu
intercourse. The reason I did not is the ultimate reason why any
us should wait. As my passion began to rise I suddenly realize
that God was in that room with me. As far as I know, the girl d
not believe in God, but I did and I knew that He was in that roor
Furthermore, God spoke to me and simply said:

> Paul you are precious to me and I love you. I have plans for
> you. I want you to help extend my Kingdom in this world. But
> to do that you must trust that I know what is best for you. An
> sex is reserved for marriage.

I can't speak for you, but for me to know that in this dark, si
world there is a God who cares for me is very special. To know th
I have meaning, to realize that there is a purpose to this universe
a marvellous thing.

And at the age of eighteen I realized those truths. I did not ha
sex before marriage because I wanted to know more of God and
be part of His plans. I wanted to share His love with others. Th
meant I was committed to living by the standards God set. A
make no mistake, it was hard. I was a healthy young ma
surrounded by friends who were losing their virginity. I know it
hard to stand up against your peer group. And with those you
people who tell me that it's sometimes hard to live God's way
agree! But that is the point. Jesus never promised that it would
easy to follow Him. To live for God means that we live by differe
priorities and standards.

If we are given the above starting point, what advice can we gi
about what is right in a relationship and how far one can go? O
can give boundaries to work within. Boundaries are helpful in th
they act as a warning. In a rugby or football match, touchlines a
the boundaries and if you go over them, it means you are out
play and the game stops. So it is in relationships. Give peop
boundaries and safe areas for them to work within. If they cro
these boundaries, warning bells should ring. In the football mat
this means that the players stop the game until the ball is back
play.

A good set of boundaries I came across was from the video *Lessons in Love* by Steve Chalke. He suggested that couples should use these four points:

- Do not lie down together
- Do not take each other's clothes off
- Do not spend long periods of time together
- Do not touch those parts of the other person's body that you do not have[31]

Now I appreciate that these boundaries are very conservative, but that is deliberate. Human nature is such that we always try to see how far we can push the boundaries. So there will be times when people step over them. Having the above boundaries will help because it will give people plenty of time to stop before they reach the point of no return. Make no mistake; there is such a point. It's the point where sexual intercourse has not taken place, but all the fires are alight in the body. This is the point of no return. It is the point of no return because this is the stage beyond which sexual intercourse is inevitable. Most people, especially young people, convince themselves that it will not happen to them - it will! Give them boundaries that stop the fire being lit.

CHAPTER 19
What about masturbation?

Amongst church-based teenagers there is one issue they always a
about – masturbation. Is it wrong? It's also a major issue among
non-churched young people.

I understand where the question has come from as I have exper
enced all the feelings and emotions they are going through. I'
known the guilt and all the drives and passions that one feels. Th
truth is the vast majority of people have been through it all – i
just that you would rather forget it. It may be you are one of th
many that try to pretend that it never occurred and therefore tre
it as a non-issue. I would suggest, however, that it's a major iss
with your teenagers. At what age it becomes an issue wi
teenagers will vary from young person to young person dependir
on when puberty begins. According to medical opinion this vari
from the age of nine to fourteen. However, the age is not the ma
issue. The issue is what is right and wrong, as so many peop
masturbate.

So where do we begin? First, by saying that the word masturb
tion sounds terrible. It sounds so harsh and wrong! I know that
may sound stupid, but the name itself does cause problems. Yo
feel bad by just saying it! You would save your children muc
difficulty if you were open and used the word in a non-emba
rassing manner. As mentioned in the earlier chapters, half th
battle is getting the issues out and talked about in a natural an
open way. Now I appreciate that talking about masturbation do
not come easily, but I think that the least you can do is be prepare
to talk about it. I recognize that this subject is one that your
people may often prefer to talk to someone else about – say a yout
leader. Even if that is the case, you should be aware of the facts.

The second thing we need to establish is the difference between false and real guilt. Real guilt is the feeling you have when you steal something. It may be that you take something from a shop without paying or you steal someone's purse. That is clearly wrong and the guilt associated with it is real and helpful. Another example of real guilt is when you wake up and don't feel like going into work, so you get your wife to telephone the office to say that you're sick. Of course, you don't feel sick but you know that the office always falls for this one. Sure enough they do, and so you stay at home. You should feel bad about that because not only did you lie, but you put your wife in a very difficult position. The guilt you feel is both real and justified.

False guilt is different. It feels the same as real guilt; the same emotional response is triggered and therefore we assume that it's justified. However, false guilt is always caused by a misunderstanding of the rights and wrongs of an issue. As an example, you may be an enthusiastic sports person and play regularly for your team. Through no fault of your own you get a cold and have to drop out of Saturday's cup match. The team lose and you feel guilty about letting the team down. This is false guilt because it was not your fault that you were ill.

As regards masturbation, there is often a lot of false guilt attached simply because all the facts are unknown. With it can come the sense of feeling dirty, of being a hypocrite and of living two lives. As young bodies develop, sexual emotions begin to be experienced that at once are pleasant but also frightening. Young people need to know what is going on and the only way they know is if they are told. We have to learn what is true guilt and what is false, but above all we need to learn to share this knowledge with young people. They need the skills to differentiate between these two states. And that is one of the roles that you have to play. Teach your children to differentiate between right and wrong.

But note carefully, not all teenagers masturbate. This makes it difficult because you must raise the issue in such a manner so as not to make those who are not masturbating feel odd.

Next, a small biology lesson. When a boy masturbates, the final outcome is a sudden increase in excitement leading to a release of semen (orgasm and ejaculation). Semen is a natural bodily

substance. Without semen you could not reproduce; it is so vit
that the male body is constantly building up a bank of it. Howeve
there is only a limited space for it in the human body so that occ
sionally when the space is full, it will empty. This, without mastu
bation, happens in your sleep and is known by most as a 'w
dream'. Even after a wet dream some young people experien
extreme guilt. This is a classic example of false guilt. Why shou
one feel guilty for what is a natural biological reaction? Do you s
the importance of talking the issues through? If you have alread
talked about this with your son, he will be more prepared when
happens. That is not to say that he may still not be disturbed by
but at least he is aware that it is a normal biological function.

Enough of the biology lesson. I remember the day I first becam
conscious that girls were not only attractive, but that I would act
ally like to hold one. Until that day I was vaguely aware of the
creatures, but frankly they were of no interest to me. Now it a
changed! I remember the day I discovered a hair on my chest.
walked round for days with my shirt undone to the navel so th
people could marvel at this! I remember the day I found whiske
on my chin – I was so proud to have my first shave. What has th
got to do with masturbation? Everything because it is all part
the journey of self-discovery. As you enter the teenage years yo
begin to discover and explore your sexuality, a process which if it
done well, has to be good. In one sense masturbation is part of t
self-discovery. However, we should recognize that it's self-centre
and therefore often referred to as solo-sex. The reason for this
that as we mature, we need to move from a position of alway
wanting to gratify our desires, our emotions and our feelings,
one of learning what true love is all about. This is a gradual proce
and is all part of having boyfriends and girlfriends and learning
begin to give love and think of others first. It is a process
learning that masturbation never really fully satisfies because it
using an orgasm in a way that was never intended. Sex is meant
be enjoyed within the security of a relationship. It is meant to
an expression between two people that satisfies bot
Masturbation can never fully satisfy because it is sex with onese
that's why I call it lonely love.

So, back to the original question – is masturbation wrong?

It could be that this is the wrong question to ask, and that we need to go one step back. When you turn to the Bible for an answer you discover a fascinating fact; it is silent on the subject of masturbation. There is no direct reference to masturbation.

This tells me a basic truth. It is not high on God's agenda of important topics. The Bible does, however, talk very specifically about acts that are wrong. For example, God is against people who misuse wealth and power. He says that neglect of parents and the abandonment of widows is wrong. The Bible is full of specific acts which God says are wrong. However, the act of masturbation is not one of them. That is why to ask if masturbation is wrong is to ask the wrong question.

To get our answer we should turn to the life of Jesus, for He spoke very practically about many issues. How about this for the standard He set for sex?

> You have heard that it was said, 'Do not commit adultery.' But now I tell you, anyone who looks at a woman and wants to possess her is guilty of committing adultery with her in his heart.   Matthew 5:27

The fascinating thing about Jesus was that He always got to the heart of the problem. The problem according to Jesus, is not so much what happens on the outside, but what is happening inside, in the mind and heart. Outward actions always start from the inside which is why it is so difficult to change human behaviour.

Here is an example of what Jesus meant. You are in bed and you begin to fantasize about the person you have fallen for and you begin to imagine what you could do with them sexually. That, according to the standards Jesus set, is wrong. It must therefore follow that if you masturbate at the same time, it's wrong. If you watch television and fantasize about your favourite film star, again according to the sex standard set by Jesus it is wrong. If you masturbate at the same time, it also follows that it is wrong.

So the issue is not directly masturbation; the issue is lifestyle and the Lordship of Jesus. Christians, however, differ in their views on this subject. Some would argue masturbation is always wrong. While I can see the validity of the argument, I do come from a slightly different position. To put it in its simplest and most practical form, if you masturbate occasionally and it's not associated with any fantasy or it's not addictive, there is not much wrong with it.

However, from my conversations with many young people I have learnt that addiction is common. Moreover, the thought life of all of us is never what it should be. So if someone is addicted to masturbation and can't stop or if they are constantly fantasizing about sex, then one has to begin to tackle the problem. The reason for this is quite simple – your body is in control of you! And it is clear from the teaching of Jesus that it's not meant to be like that. When we follow Jesus we need to realize that we are not alone, but that Jesus through the Holy Spirit is living in us. Being a follower of Jesus means that we listen to what he tells us: 'His commandments are not too hard . . . for . . . every child of God is able to defeat the world . . . by means of our faith.' (1 John 5:3–4) We are called to live a life that Jesus would be pleased with because He has given us a changed heart, new love and the power to live it through the Holy Spirit. We are meant to be people who are living lives that will change and challenge those around us. That simply means being in control of our thoughts and emotions.

CHAPTER 20
What about homosexuality?

There is one thing I'm asked about wherever I go: what do I think about homosexuality? Yet there probably is no other subject that so divides people. I have included this chapter only because people want an answer. You may not agree with what I have to say, but I tackle the issue because your children want to know about it. I also recognize that Christians differ over their views on this subject, but the following is my own view. You may not agree with it but I hope that it will provoke you to think the matter through and to have an opinion accordingly.

The young man was getting very heated and it was obvious he couldn't contain his thoughts any longer. 'All homosexuals are perverts and should be shot,' he finally shouted. Was this a view expressed in some extreme right-wing pressure group meeting? No, it was a sixth-form debate in an average British school. Homosexuality is *the* subject that always arouses strong passions and views in sixth-form discussions. What is very sad and surprising is that the above view is often expressed and supported by a large minority of young people. Other views range from, 'As it's not my problem, it does not bother me,' to 'It's a free society and people should be free to choose their sexual partners'.

It is an issue that causes much pain, not the least to homosexuals. In our culture most people have a deep-seated fear of homosexuals – the formal term is homophobia. Many would deny this, but if you scratch the surface, you would find underneath that the fear is in most of us.

I have sat with young people as they have shared their confusion about homosexuality. I have also listened as some have shared their confusion about their own sexuality. They wonder if they might be homosexual. What are they to do? Where do they go for help? These are big issues that need to be handled with love and care.

I remember the day it was announced that I would speak at large church about homosexuality. I have never forgotten th phone calls that followed. 'You can't speak at our church on tha subject,' one very distressed person remarked, 'afterall childre will be present.' There was genuine horror that we should b talking about such a subject in the first place. The fact that chi dren would be present only made matters worse.

The comments and attitudes expressed disturbed me for number of reasons. First, there was, and is, such incredible igno rance on the subject. And, sadly, ignorance often leads to fear an intolerance in many situations in life. Racism is a classic example an evil that has many of its roots based in ignorance. The same pre udice is certainly true with regard to homosexuality. As I listened t people arguing their reasons for not speaking on the topic, I coul smell, sense and hear ignorance. Their views and fears were based o wrong information or no information. 'All homosexuals are chil molesters' or 'Homosexuality is the cause of declining standards i our country' or 'AIDS is God's judgement on homosexuals'. Thes were just some sort of the distorted views I have heard.

The second thing that disturbed me about the comments wa the pain that such attitudes must bring to those with homosexua orientation. The way the comments are made often makes homo sexuals feel of less value than animals. Views are expressed with great deal of anger and hatred. Not only does this cause great hur to homosexuals but reinforces their views about Christians and th Church. Study the life of Jesus – He never once spoke to anyone i such a manner. Certainly He always spoke the truth and at time some of His sayings are very hard, but the heart of Jesus is alway love. Jesus always demonstrated the true value of people in the wa that He talked and dealt with them. This is a quality that many us fail to show time and time again.

Although, therefore, our culture may be homophobic, th Church needs to set a radical alternative. Unfortunately it has to often failed! So the first thing we need to do is repent of ou obvious homophobia. Richard Lovelace summed the issue u when he said:

> Most of the repenting that needs to be done on this issue of homosexuality needs to be done by straight people, including straight Christians. By far the greater sin in our Church is the sin of neglect, fear, hatred, just wanting to brush these people under the rug.[32]

In repenting of our attitude we're not ignoring that the Bible teaches that the physical act in homosexuality is wrong. Rather we are acknowledging that we have been wrong to make value judgements based on a person's orientation. This has to be the heart of the issue. Judgements are often made about homosexuals on the basis of orientation and not on behaviour.

Orientation vs. Behaviour

A male heterosexual's natural inclination is towards women. A homosexual, however, is sexually attracted to someone of their own sex. That is their orientation. To make value judgements based on a person's orientation is wrong. For example, take the average male heterosexual who is attracted towards women. There is nothing wrong with that. However, if they have an affair, that is wrong; if they have sex with a prostitute, that is wrong; if they have sex outside marriage, that is wrong. Those judgements are made on the person's behaviour, not orientation. The orientation is not wrong; it's how one chooses to express it that is the issue. So it is with homosexuals. Their natural inclination is an attraction towards the same sex and it is my understanding that the Bible does not condemn that. The fact that heterosexuals find this hard to accept does not make it wrong. It's the physical act of homosexual sex that is wrong.

This book is not meant to be a biblical exposition. Rather it is intended to be a practical help based on biblical truth. There are seven biblical references to homosexuality. Please note that is only seven references. Now don't get me wrong; even if there was only one reference the truth would be the same. However there are over 300 references to abuse and misuse of money in scripture. I think it would be right to say that the Church's attitude towards the abuse of money is not the same as it is towards homosexuality. It is this sort of contradiction that we need to be aware of when tackling the topic with young people for they would be quick to observe it.

As far as I can see, the Bible points to the truth that the act of sex between a man and a man or a woman and a woman is wrong. This may sound hard in our so-called liberated 90s, but so is the truth that sexual intercourse is meant to be enjoyed within the confines of marriage. These are truths that God has established for our well-being and we are wise to listen to Him.

Where do we go now?

So where does this leave us? With the reality that some people have a homosexual orientation. Whether it's due to conditioning or genes or a combination of both is still open to debate. The truth remains that some people are more attracted to people of the same sex. The Bible does not condemn people for their orientation. Trouble has occurred because most people have equated the sexual act with the orientation. They see that the Bible condemns the sexual act and, therefore, they can also condemn the orientation. This leads to the conclusion that homosexuals are in the wrong, which is clearly unbiblical and wrong itself. A homosexual is as much a sinner as you and I are and the truth of the Bible is that God loves us all. The Bible clearly states: 'For God so loved the world He gave . . .' It does not say, as some imply, 'For God so loved the world, except for homosexuals'. The biblical truth is that Jesus loves all of humanity, not just a select few.

So, to people with a homosexual orientation, you need to hear that God loves you. That is not to say that He approves of your life style if you are living outside His commands; He does not. But He still loves you.

What are the major issues facing teenagers?

John is thirteen and he is very aware that he is more attracted to boys than girls. He is very confused and anxious. Does this mean that he is a homosexual? Probably not. It is just a phase through which the vast majority of young people go. In the book *Childhood and Adolescence* the psychologist, J. Hadfield, recognizes three periods that all teenagers pass through:

- Puberty – twelve to fourteen: this is typified by the gang spirit and rapid development of psychological sex functions.
- Transition period – fifteen: passing from a homosexual to a heterosexual phase.
- Later adolescence – sixteen plus: characterized by heterosexuality and ideals.

According to psychologists, the phase that concerns teenagers and homosexuality is the puberty and transition period when there is a very strong loyalty to members of the same sex. Bonding at this age is very strong and hence it is difficult for a newcomer to break into the group. It is also the stage when strong links are made with teachers. As young people move from puberty to the transition period they become very moody and will have nothing to do with the opposite sex. Interestingly at this stage children often have a very strong loyalty to the opposite parent. So a boy will be very loyal to the mother and a girl very loyal to her father and she can become very jealous of her mother.

Now that is a very short and simplified explanation. It does however highlight what can be a major problem. There is no doubt that there is a time in a teenager's life where he or she is more attracted to the same sex. This does not mean that he or she is a homosexual, rather it's a part of the growing-up process. The last thing that young people need during this period are messages which confuse them. It is for this reason that the role of 'gender benders' of the 80s must be questioned. Artists like Boy George and Eurhythmics have produced many songs and videos. A number of them have created a real sense of the merging of sexes. The videos they produced often mixed the gender roles leading to confusion about who you were really attracted to. The image created was such that you did not know if you were attracted to the woman who was played by a man who really turned out to be a man playing a woman dressed up as a man. Confused? That's the idea. The artists, of course, in writing the songs were using parody a great deal and were also tackling some very real issues. However, the average 12 to 14-year-old does not recognize parody, let alone understand it. What he understands is what he sees. So he is given a very confused message about sexuality. Rather than liberating

him, as is intended, it actually causes more pain and anguish. M
concern over the 'gender benders' is not so much for the perso
who has the homosexual orientation, but rather for the teenage
who is led to believe that he has because of all these differen
images. As we have seen, young people will go through a stag
where they are attracted to the same sex; this does not make then
homosexual. However, some of the images may push them into
lifestyle they do not want. It is these people who later become ver
confused because they have taken on an identity that was neve
theirs.

Steps to positive action

1 The sexual act in a homosexual relationship is a wrong. But
so is the sexual act in a heterosexual relationship outside
marriage. The way some people talk, they make the
homosexual act seem worse than any other. It is not. If you
are a homosexual your lustful thoughts and acts are a wrong
but equally so is any lust, bitterness, pride or jealousy that I
might have.

2 We need to remember that there is an amazing diversity in
humanity. We are not meant to be stereotypes that follow
one another like clones. Some women are more masculine
than others and some men more feminine. It is great that we
have moved from the days where in school boys did
woodwork and metalwork while girls did cookery and
sewing. Nowadays schools are fully integrated in these
subjects which is healthy for it will break down some of our
sexual stereotyping. My hope is that you will allow your
children to be who they are. So if your son reads poetry, likes
cookery and is very sensitive, rejoice in that and encourage
him. If your daughter wants to play football and enjoys car
mechanics, encourage her because that is who she is.

3 The Church must become an environment which helps those
with a homosexual orientation to feel supported and helped.
For those who are committed to living a celibate life, it can
be incredibly lonely and frustrating. We need to understand
their pain and help them through it. Only by God's grace

can each of us live a day at a time. Some homosexuals want to change – to be heterosexual. There is evidence that healing can take place and that they marry women. I have known one such person. For the majority of homosexuals change does not take place and they spend the rest of their lives living with the situation. We need to offer understanding. We need to create a community for them to find support.

4 We can help by becoming friends with them. By being people they can talk with about their fears and hopes. They want companions they can trust. The Church should be this place. The Church should be the place where they discover warm, unconditional love.

suspect that my child is a homosexual – what should I do?

First you must be slow to come to a judgement about this. What is it that has led to this belief? It may be that he is seventeen and still has not had a girlfriend. There is nothing wrong with that. Some people develop later than others. It may be that your son is not keen on committing himself to a person. It could be that he is not interested in having a partner and that he is very happy staying single. The problem is that we are too preoccupied with sexual relationships in our culture.

My son is a homosexual – what should I do?

The first and most important thing you can do is to love him. However deep your disappointment, even if you feel revulsion for something that you thought impossible – love him. How you respond to your son is of vital importance. Rejection at this point will cause lasting damage. Remember what I said earlier about God's love for all humanity. You need to demonstrate that to your child. You need to love him.

Also remember that it has taken a great deal of courage for him to tell you. Your son will have gone through many months, if not years of torment, coming to terms with his sexuality. He will be very scared about telling you. This for him is his worst moment. Your own parents are the hardest people to tell. And he has done that. So recognize the courage that has been shown.

You will need to take time. Don't blame him. Don't ask i
you've failed. These are issues that you can tackle later. Right now
– just love him. I appreciate that for many this may be hard. Yo
may be in shock. If you are homophobic, everything inside yo
will want to deny it. To reach out and love your son is possibly th
last thing that you want or can do. It's wise at this point t
remember that love is an act of the will. It's not some emotiona
feeling that makes you feel good. It is an act of will. It is somethin,
you commit yourself to do. Sometimes love means that we press o
even when everything inside us screams stop! Of course, it is als
when the grace of God begins to work. In our weakness w
discover the power of God's love. So for those of us who believe, w
are not alone in this. There is a God who will give us the grace t
deal with the situation a day at a time.

In all probability you will not be able to talk all the issue.
through with your son. I suggest that a good counsellor or youth
worker is called in. Your son is going to need support. He does no
need to be ostracized further.

CHAPTER 21
Will I ever find love?

Wherever we do *The Seduction* presentation, they will always be here, sitting at the back of the hall. They may look, speak and dress differently, but they are still the same. Who are they? The lads! The boys! They are the ones who walk into the hall with great confidence. Everything about their body language is challenging me, saying, 'Try telling us something we don't already know.' These lads are 'cool' and streetwise; they've seen it all, done it all and been there. In other words, they know it all. However, there is a part of *The Seduction* presentation when all their pretence goes. At this point they are with me because the words I'm speaking touch something, deep inside. It occurs when I quote the following line from a Martyn Joseph song.

> We don't know nothing, we don't know much, just an aching
> and a longing to be loved.[33]

There is another character always at the presentations and again he is easy to spot. He is easy to spot because he sits by himself. I know that other children are on either side of him but he's by himself – he's got no friends. He shuffles in with shirt hanging loose and trousers that look as if they've been slept in. Nobody wants to be his friend, so he just sits and waits. There is no life in him. It's as if somebody has switched the lights off and gone home. But again it's those same words that get a reaction from him:

> We don't know nothing, we don't know much, just an aching
> and a longing to be loved.

At that point something inside him comes alive as if a light has been switched on. Occasionally our eyes meet and I can see the question he has: 'Please, can I really be loved?'

And a certain kind of girl is always there. Most, but not all. She is the envy of her year and every boy wants to go out with her. She is stunningly attractive and everybody assumes life is easy for her. After all she has the pick of the boys, but strangely she is rarely seen with one. She has many friends but none of them suspect her problem. As I speak, she too comes alive when I make the statement:

> We don't know nothing, we don't know much, just an aching
> and a longing to be loved.

Beautiful she may be to others but to herself she is ugly. She thinks that she's of no value. She, too, wonders about the possibility that someone may love her for who she is rather than how she looks.

The list of people could go on, but one thing is true. One thing I am certain of. Deep in the heart of all of us is the desire to be loved. It is true irrespective of colour, creed or religion. You can't measure this need in some laboratory; there is not a part of the anatomy that represents it, but there is a mystical something inside all of us that cries out to be loved. It can't be bought, it can't be operated on, but there is a great need for it to be met.

It's locked away in a secret room in our soul. We occasionally take a look, but that can be painful so we lock it away and pretend it's not there. The trouble is that you may lock it up, but it still affects all you are. This desire is so powerful in all of us that it affects all we do. It affects our personality, how we respond to others and the partner we choose. To know we are loved is fundamental to all of us.

Peter Gabriel sang about this need for love on his album *US*:

> So, you know how people are/When it's all gone much too
> far/The way their minds are made.
> Still, there's something you should know/That I could not let
> show/That fear of letting go,
> And in this moment, I need to be needed/With this darkness

all around me, I like to be liked./In the emptiness and fear, I
want to be wanted./Cos I love to be loved/I love to be loved.[34]

Madonna is an icon to millions of young people and is seen as
somebody who is not afraid to express her sexuality. Using parody
in her music and videos she pushes sexual innuendo to the limit.
At times her live shows border on the pornographic. Despite all
this outward confidence the following comment made by her
suggests that she, too, recognizes this universal need for love:

> My mother died when I was really young and all I really knew
> about her was that she was very innocent and very religious .
> . . I never knew that she actually liked me. I guess I'm still
> seeking her approval so I go to stadiums seeking it . . . but
> you can never really escape your past.[35]

'I never knew my mother actually liked me . . .' I think that's her
guarded way of saying love.

A student came up to me after I had given a talk on the basic
human need for love. This is what he said:

> What you have just said is true. My father has never hugged
> me and I've been out with a whole string of girlfriends simply
> because I am looking for someone to love me.

It is this need for love that has convinced me that the issue of sex is
not primarily about biology.

Sex as a god

Certainly we need to know the basics. We need to be educated
about the practical issues. But the real issue of sex, the subject at
the heart of it, is love – the fundamental need of our lives. The
tragedy is that we are living in a culture that has elevated sex to a
position in which it is never meant to be.

Victor Frankl is an Austrian psychotherapist who recognizes the
danger of this position. Frankl accepts that much of our modern
understanding of sex and sexuality comes from the work of

Sigmund Freud. It was Freud who wrote three papers which became a bench-mark on the subject. One of Freud's theories was that man's greatest drive is the 'will for pleasure', in particular the sex drive. It is this, he postulated, that motivates and drives man. In other words sex is a major influence on our being.

Frankl, however, disagrees with Freud's observation mainly because of his experience during the Second World War when he spent time in Auschwitz concentration camp. He noticed two things.

First, if sex is one of man's greatest drives, why was it that in the camp nobody was having sex? If sex was such a major drive, people would have it whatever their circumstances. They did not have sex because it wasn't the major drive. The problem is that the forces which shape our modern culture, advertising, music, television and films, have made it to be so. The way they've projected sex has made it to be the fundamental of life. And we've bought into it. People are having sex because the image that is tattooed on their mind tells them it will deliver love.

Frankl made a second observation about life in the camp. Looking back he noticed that there were a few, like himself, who survived the horror. Amongst those who survived he noticed a common thread — they all had something to believe in that was beyond themselves. While in the camp they were able to believe in something that was beyond the perimeter fence. For some it was a wife, husband, grandparent, son or daughter; for others it was a business or project. Whatever it was, it was something outside themselves.

It was this observation that became the foundation of all his work. People need a reason outside themselves in which to believe. The difficulty, he observed, is that we are living in an increasingly fragmenting and dysfunctional society. Crime is increasing, families do not work as they once did, and the gap between those who have and those who do not is widening. The ever increasing development of technology is alienating more and more people. A major consequence of this fragmentation is that people no longer have anything to believe in. Technology seems to be failing, families don't work, jobs are no longer for life and God is supposedly dead; what, therefore, is there left to believe in?

In short we are living in a culture that has lost its identity and its security. There are many consequences of this loss, but one of the fundamental ones is that it leads to sex taking a place for which it was never created. Frankl went on to say this about modern culture:

> In a society with no meaning to life, libido (sexual desire) will run rampant in the search for pain killers and emotional analgesics.[36]

The fundamental need at the centre of our being is the need to be loved. The heart of love is intimacy and security. Intimacy is the ability to feel at one with another human being, the knowledge that you are not alone and the deep certainty that you are loved. Security is the knowledge that you are in safe hands and that ultimately there is a purpose to this universe. Frankl contends that as society loses its meaning, it will turn to sex and make it into something it never was meant to be.

Sexual intercourse is uniquely the most intimate way you will ever get to know somebody. It can also be for a few fleeting moments the most secure you ever feel. This shouldn't surprise us because God created sex to be enjoyed within the framework of marriage where it is meant to bring intimacy and security.

It should not surprise us then that people have sex because for a few fleeting moments it can bring security and intimacy. But it is only for a few moments. When sex is made the foundation of a relationship, it will end in failure. Sex was not designed to accomplish that. Sex is meant to be an expression of love. Sex is meant to be an expression of things that already exist in the relationship – intimacy and security. Let's not sell young people short with the lie that sex brings security and love. It does not.

Our teenagers, indeed all of us, are sold short if we perpetuate the myth that sex alone can meet this deep need of ours. Sex can be an expression of love, but it is not the same as the deep satisfying love we all desperately want. I am not talking here of love that leads to marriage but rather of a love that all human beings want to experience. That's what Madonna, Peter Gabriel and all the others quoted above meant.

This universal desire for love is a major theme in the Bible. It shows that at the heart of this universe there is a God who loves us. He knows our inner being. He has heard our worst thought, seen our darkest moment and yet still loves us. It is true that there is a God in this universe who loves you and me.

> O Lord, you have searched me and you know me. You know when I sit and when I rise; you perceive my thoughts from afar. You discern my going out and my lying down; you are familiar with all my ways. Before a word is on my tongue you know it completely, O Lord. You hem me in – behind and before; you have laid your hand upon me. Such knowledge is too wonderful for me, too lofty for me to attain.   *Psalm 139*

As Karl Barth so movingly explains it:

> God loved us before anyone did.
> He loves us better than anyone.
> He'll love us long after everyone else has forgotten us.

The heart of humanity is to know that we are loved. Many things in life can partly fulfil that desire – partner, children and friends. Many things can mask the desire – sex, money, power, prestige. There is, however, only one person who can truly satisfy that desire – God. To know the love of God is to be at peace. To know the love of God is to be secure. To know the love of God is to experience intimacy. I am convinced that the answer to our deepest needs is an encounter with the love of God.

CHAPTER 22

Weapon four

The battle for the spirit – supporting your children through the power of prayer

My wife remembers as a young girl her mother getting up early ever morning. When she asked her what she was doing, her mother explained that she got up early every morning to pray for her. My wife's mother got up early every day of her life to pray for her daughters. I am convinced that's had a major effect on my wife's life. It has protected her from many negative influences on her life. I can't stress how important I think the place of prayer is. You can read all the books on culture, develop an ABC of tackling the teenage crisis, but unless prayer is at the top you will have limited success. One of the greatest gifts you can give to your children is the commitment to pray for them every day.

Our problem in the West is that we've become a very active generation and so when faced with a difficulty or problem, we tend to react by going into action. We want books to read, a seven-step plan of action or a seminar to attend. The central teaching of the Bible is that first we should pray. It was an example that Jesus gave all His life. Time and time again we find that Jesus went off to pray. When He was faced by major decisions in His life he went away and prayed.

Prayer is vital because the battle we are in is not only to do with what we can see. Paul wrote about this in the Bible:

> Finally, be strong in the Lord, and in the strength of His might. Put on the full armour of God, that you may be able to stand firm against the schemes of the devil. For our struggle is not against flesh and blood, but against the rulers, against the powers, against the world-forces of this darkness, against the spiritual forces of wickedness in the heavenly places.

> Therefore, take up the full armour of God, that you may be
> able to resist in the evil day, and having done everything,
> stand firm.   *Ephesians 6:10–13*

Paul talks about powers and principalities. By that he means governments and people in power. But he is also talking about another dimension, he is talking about the spiritual powers that affect us. Paul is deliberately ambiguous because he wants us to realize that both options are a reality and affect us. It is true that those in 'powerful positions' seek to rob our children of their innocence.

But there is no doubt that there is also a spiritual dimension to all this. Satan's desire is to rob each and every one of us of our inheritance – a relationship with God. It means we are in a battle and the weapon of this battle is prayer. It is your responsibility as a parent to pray for your children. Prayer is the first and greatest weapon that we have in fighting the cultural war. You need to commit yourself to praying for your children.

Action Points

- Make a promise to pray for your children every day.
- Consider meeting regularly with two or three friends to pray for each other's children. This could become a very valuable source of support.
- If you are interested in young people, you could start praying for your local schools and youth clubs. Find out all you can so that you are praying about the right things.
- If you belong to a local church talk to your youth leader. Ask him or her what issues concerning young people need praying about. Consider starting a prayer group for the youth of the church.
- If you want to learn about young people, I suggest three things. First, go to your local newsagent and buy a selection of teenage magazines. Read them at home and ask what tattoos they are leaving on young people's minds. Second, watch a selection of children's TV including some of the music programmes. Go to your local music store and simply

browse and listen. Third, talk to children! A simple suggestion, but one that many adults seem to find intimidating. They are only human! Make the effort and you will not be disappointed.

- Although hard, I suggest that you examine your lifestyle. What is a priority in your life? What do all your energies go into? Does your lifestyle challenge others? These are big questions that all of us need to be constantly asking if we are to change the lives of others.

- Young people often appreciate a place they can drop in to. They like a place with a sense of community. Not many are called or are gifted enough to organize such a place. But if you sense this is what you want to do – let me encourage you – do it! There is a great need for small communities that support young people.

PART THREE
A Better Way to Live

My mother died when I was really young and all I really knew about her was that she was very innocent and very religious . . . I never knew that she actually liked me. I guess I'm still seeking her approval so I go to stadiums seeking it . . . but you can never really escape your past. *Madonna*

So, you know how people are/When it's all gone much too far/The way their minds are made.
Still, there's something you should know/That I could not let show/That fear of letting go,
And in this moment, I need to be needed/With this darkness all around me, I like to be liked./In the emptiness and fear, I want to be wanted./'Cos I love to be loved/I love to be loved. *Peter Gabriel*

A lot of people are always concerned about: 'How can I help people? Or help the youth come to Christ? Or preach well?' But these are basically non-issues. If you are burning with the love of Jesus, don't worry: everyone will know. They will say, 'I want to get close to this person who is so full of God.'[37] *Henri Nouwen*

CHAPTER 23
What if they should let you down?

You are in the middle of cooking the supper when your daughter comes home. Her eyes are red and look very sore; mascara is streaked down her face. With great concern you ask, 'What's the matter, darling?' With that your daughter bursts into long, deep sobs and somehow between the deep gasps for air, she blurts out, 'I'm pregnant!' Your world is about to change . . . what do you do?

Your son comes home from school. All night he is on edge. You try everything to get him to talk. Nothing works. Finally at 11.30p.m. he shouts, 'Sarah's pregnant'. He stands there almost challenging you to do something. To react in the way that he expects. Your world is about to change . . . what do you do?

The examples could go on in life after life. The misuse of sex has broken hearts, friendships, businesses, families and churches. The hurt it has inflicted on lives is immeasurable. The misuse of sex is probably responsible for more broken lives than anything else. At this very moment there are thousands of people who are asking one question. Is there any hope? Yes!

First, as I travel and talk with people I have noticed that many are beginning to tire of the misuse of sex. People are beginning to realize that it does not deliver all that it has claimed to. In fact most people feel that they are on a treadmill. They are tired of sexual adventures that, after the initial thrill, fail to satisfy. If people were not so tired by life they would be looking for alternative options. But people are just weary and tired. There is no energy left. It may not sound very hopeful, but it is ! To realize that sex does not delivery everything is a big step in the right direction.

The second reason for hope is to be found in the greatest quality all of us need – forgiveness. Forgiveness can be the bridge that brings healing to deep hurts, that allows God's Spirit to move in new ways. Forgiveness has the power to mend broken relationships, to bring joy back and breathe new life into tired empty lives. Forgiveness is the heart of the Christian message. It is meant to be at the heart of our experience and no more so than in the area of sex and sexuality.

Forgiveness gives us hope that there will be new starts. Your world is about to change. You are faced by a son or daughter who has just told you that they've got it wrong. They are broken and hurt. They need to know that it's not the end of the road for them. They need to hear that there are new beginnings. Right now you may feel that's impossible. At this very moment all the dreams and plans you had for your child are shattered. As for them, they are devastated and what they need right now is your forgiveness. What they need at their moment of crisis is not another lecture. They just want to be embraced by you and know that you love them and forgive them. You may find that hard to do. Everything inside you is hurting. You have many mixed emotions and questions. You will begin to deal with these over the next days and weeks. But right now what they need most is your forgiveness. That's where the healing begins.

First . . . an apology

Before going further into the issue of forgiveness we need to realize a hard truth. The vast majority of people are of the opinion that the Church is the last place to go to find forgiveness. This has come about because of the way the Church has often dealt with those who have got it wrong sexually. As a teenager I remember desperately wanting to talk to someone about the problem of heavy petting and masturbation. I needed help so that I could work out what was wrong and what was acceptable. I was, however, too scared to approach anybody in the Church because I felt that at best they would laugh at me and at the worst condemn me. It therefore meant that I spent my teenage years confused and hurt because I had no one to talk with.

The sadness is that those days have not changed. As I talk to many young people one thing is very clear, they are broken and want help. The tragedy is that they don't turn to the Church because they feel they will be judged and rejected. We need to reclaim the Church as a vibrant place that offers healing to the broken. It does not mean that we sacrifice what we believe to be right and wrong, but rather that we start to operate as Jesus did.

It also means that forgiveness is not one way. God loves us and wants to pour His healing love into our lives. For that to become a reality we need to do something. We need to acknowledge our wrong and accept God's forgiveness. If we have had an affair we confess the wrongness of it to our partner and to God. If we have sex outside marriage we need to confess to God that it was wrong. In whatever way we get it wrong we need to acknowledge it. It is a two-way affair. God will forgive us but we need to ask for it.

Forgiveness was always the way Jesus operated. He couldn't have been more clear about His attitude to sin, and yet people such as prostitutes, adulterers and those who slept around always felt that they could approach Him. Because in Jesus they discovered someone who would accept them for who they were and begin to discuss the hurts and difficulties they were facing. And as they talked with Him they discovered that there was a God who could bring wholeness and forgiveness into their lives. A forgiveness that they wanted because they could see the wrongness of their actions.

So we need to apologize for a Church that has got it wrong in this whole sexual arena. We need to apologize for a Church that has made it incredibly difficult for teenagers to talk openly and honestly about their feelings, joy, pain and frustrations. They don't talk about these issues because they feel they'll be condemned. So let us be honest and admit that we have got it wrong. We need to seek out those that we have offended by our attitudes to their wrongdoing and ask their forgiveness. It will be hard to do, but it will be the beginning of something new and wonderful in our churches.

Don't despair

So please, do not despair, there is a God of love who does listen, who does accept people for who they are and who wants to bring His forgiveness into their life. There is great hope. All is not lost. If you are a parent or someone who is dealing with one of the broken, give them hope. The chance is that they will feel a failure. They will believe that what they have done is beyond help and hope. The good news is that there is hope and there are new beginnings as that is what Jesus is all about. You will need to remind people time and time again that God still loves them. There is nothing that they have done which will separate them from His love. Hold on to that truth in the dark days.

The mob and the failure

A mob of men brought a woman to Jesus. They'd caught her in the act of adultery and now they claimed the legal right to stone her. It was the law of the day that those caught committing adultery should be stoned to death. Jesus, however, does not answer them straight away. Rather He kneels down and begins writing on the ground. We do not know what He wrote; I however like to think that it was the Ten Commandments – do not kill, honour your mother and father, do not commit adultery, etc. He then stood up and said to the mob, 'The person who has never done anything wrong; pick up the first stone and throw it.' Again He bent down and wrote in the dust. One by one these men looked at the commandments, then looked at their names and slowly they began to realize that they were just as guilty as the woman. In all probability they had not committed adultery, but they had told lies, gossiped, slandered people, treated the poor badly and so on. They realized that they were as guilty as the woman. So one by one they began to walk away until the woman was left alone at the feet of Jesus.

Jesus then did an incredible thing. He lifted the woman up and then the Bible says this:

> The woman was left alone. Jesus stood up and spoke to her.
> 'Woman, where are they? Does no one condemn you?'
> 'No one, Master.'
> 'Neither do I,' said Jesus. 'Go on your way. From now on, don't sin.'

John 8:10, 11

Get hold of that. Jesus did not condemn her. The church would, but Jesus did not! Neither did He agree with what she had done, for He told her not to do it again. What she had done was clearly wrong. Rather Jesus forgave her. This woman's life was in a mess. Her emotions would have been shattered. She would be full of guilt and in all probability felt a failure. At that very moment she would have felt that there was no hope. But there was! In forgiving her Jesus took away all the guilt, shame and pain that this woman was experiencing.

Dealing with guilt

That is the power of forgiveness; it deals with the guilt. Guilt is at the heart of all our brokenness. Dealing with guilt is a major priority. The problem is that many do not seem to know how to resolve the problem. This dilemma was recognized by the author, Tom Wolfe. He is probably most famous for the book *Bonfire of the Vanities*. He recognized the problem of guilt in our culture with this observation:

> When Nietzsche said that God is dead, he said there would have to be created a new set of values to replace the values of Christianity. God was dead, *but guilt was not, and there was no way to absolve it.*[38]

Our culture, he remarked, declared that God is dead. One of the consequences of this position is that there is no way left for dealing with people's guilt. Who now can bring forgiveness? Who can deal with all the effects? That is why we have so many broken lives. People are no longer able to find forgiveness. Woody Allen's film *Crimes and Misdemeanours* deals powerfully with the issue of unresolved guilt. The film is about whether somebody can get away with and live with murder. He commits the crime and does get away with it, but the film becomes darker and darker as the end approaches. Yes, he got away with murder, but he is left with a real darkness in his life which affects everything he does.

That is what unresolved guilt does. It affects our whole being. Sometimes we push it away, but all that happens is that it gets locked into some dark dungeon in our soul. We think it's gone away, but the reality is that we are chained to it. Every so often the chain in the dungeon gives us a tug just to remind us that it's there. What are we to do with guilt?

Our culture may not offer any hope, but Jesus does. So to all those people who ask whether there is hope for a new start – yes, there is, because Jesus demonstrated it time and time again with the people He met. For some it will be an instantaneous experience and for others it will be a gradual process that takes time. The important factor, however, is that it is possible.

We need to grasp the enormity of God's forgiveness. That is what the parable of the Prodigal Son is all about. It is a father who does not glower when his son fails, but rather searches the horizon, desperate for any sign of his wayward child. It is the father who runs to the son, throws his arms around him and kisses him. That's the breathtaking quality of God's forgiveness. And that is what we need to bring to the lives of young people and indeed all of us because it is desperately needed.

Questions that demand an answer

As you talk with young people, they will throw up a whole range of questions that they desperately want answers for:

> Can the guilt of what I have done ever be taken away?

> I've gone too far with my boyfriend or girlfriend; will God ever forgive me?

> I slept with somebody last night – can I get my virginity back?

> My father abused me as a 5-year-old and since then my whole life has been a jumble of emotions, shame, guilt, hatred, confusion; can I learn to love again?

These are real questions from real people in real situations and you need to reassure them on three levels.

First, they're not alone or unusual. Thousands of teenagers

around the country are asking many of the same questions. It is perfectly normal in today's world that this is so. Part of the relief for many is knowing that their problem is not unique. To realize that others are going through the same thing will help – so reassure them.

Second, remind them how much God loves them for who they are. His love does not depend on what we have or have not done, however we feel. We may feel utter contempt for ourselves. God does not. All our emotions scream at us, 'You are a nobody.' God does not. There is nothing that we have done or will do that can stop God loving us. Furthermore, He cries with our pain and confusion because it is not the way it is meant to be.

Third, being a Christian is no guarantee that you will not face the same problems and difficulties. Being a Christian does not mean we will not ever fail again. We do! We just have to get up and begin again.

Real forgiveness

So how do we find or help others to find God's forgiveness? The heart of forgiveness is the cross of Jesus. The cross is God's reminder that forgiveness is always available.

We also need to appreciate that there are many degrees of getting it wrong and that some lives will be more hurt and messed up than others. For some it will be simply that they've just fooled around a little and crossed a few boundaries; for others it is the pain of losing their virginity and for others the deep hurt from having been raped or abused. Each needs to experience the forgiveness of God, but with vastly different levels of help. Each needs to know that Jesus cries with their pain and for the life messed up by a misuse of the gift of sex.

For some there will be the need to seek out the aid of an experienced counsellor who will help the person discover the depth and width of God's love. A book is really not the place to turn to for help. We need friends and in all probability we need people with experience in these areas who will spend time working through the issues.

My hope is that the Church will again become a refuge for the broken. It will become a place where people experience the breath-taking freedom that forgiveness brings. I want it to be a place where young people can talk openly and honestly about their problems without fear of condemnation or rejection.

Creating that place starts with me and you. We have to learn to forgive one another and to be a reflection of God's love. It means that you must forgive your teenagers if they mess up sexually or in any other area. You can be the greatest indicator of God's love to your children. The way you treat them will be an indication of the way God treats us. That is the exciting challenge of it all.

CHAPTER 24
A better way

There is no doubt that warnings, boundaries and exhortations are vital in helping to protect our children. That said, the negative can only ever be part of the answer. The very best way in which to influence the lives of your children is to put before them positively a goal for their lives – a better way.

Two of my best friends are very successful doctors. Yet five years ago I stood at Heathrow airport waving to them as they walked into the departure lounge and into a whole new life. They had given up their jobs and were flying off to work in a Third-World country. In doing that they were giving up financial security. Although their new positions are paid, the salary is considerably less than for the equivalent job in this country. They have given up a nice house, a big car and a Western lifestyle. Why have they done that? What possessed them to do such a thing?

It's Sunday night, it's raining, it's cold and it's miserable. Yet in the town centre a group of about eighty people are congregating around a barbecue stand. These men and women are wrapped up in all sorts of clothes. Coats that are too big and jackets that are too small; hats and gloves are of all colours and sizes. Many are sniffing and most are coughing. These are just some of the homeless who gather here every two weeks. This is the time when a few people have got together and prepared some hot food for them. They have also collected second-hand clothing and they smile as the homeless try on different garments. But think for a minute. It's a Sunday night when most people are at home watching television or visiting friends. It's normally a time when most people are relaxing ready for Monday morning and work. So why have these people given this up to stand in the rain and feed the homeless?

To answer that let me ask *you* a question? What is it that attracted people to Jesus? Why is it that for three years people were prepared to give up their work and homes and follow this man? What was it about Him that people found so attractive? Countless books have been written on this subject with many good and valid reasons. There was, however, one thing that Jesus demonstrated which was a major influence in people's decision-making process. It was simply that Jesus demonstrated the truth – there is a better way to live. People came to listen to Jesus and to watch how He dealt with others. And as they watched they saw that life had much more to offer than they were experiencing. Their lives were poor compared with the riches Jesus offered.

That's the reason my friends gave up their secure jobs and flew off to a Third-World country; they wanted to show that there is a better way to live. It is why people gave out food and clothes to the homeless; they wanted to show that there is a better way to live. It is a belief that this world is not the only one that exists. Rather there is another world, God's Kingdom, where there are different standards and values. To show the better way is to live out the reality of this Kingdom.

The people were attracted to Jesus, they followed Him and listened to His every word because He came to show and explain that there was a better way. In theological language it is known as the Kingdom of God – the active reign of God. Time and time again Jesus showed the power and the reality of the Kingdom. Jesus' life showed that there was more to this life than the world we live in. This is how the writer, T.S. Eliot, explained it:

> To believe in the supernatural is not simply to believe that after living a successful, material and fairly virtuous life here one will continue to exist in the best possible substitute for this world, or that after living a starved and stunted life here one will be compensated with all the good things one has gone without: it is to believe that the supernatural is the greatest reality here and now!

Now I'm not certain where T.S. Eliot stood as regards the faith, but what he is saying is this. If the supernatural means anything, it must not be just some pie in the sky when I die. Rather the reality of the supernatural must be seen here and now. It's a life that is governed by different standards; it's a life that has different priorities. It's a life that is lived out in faith that there is a God who affects the here and now. It is a life that must invade all that we are in terms of our personality, our lifestyle and our work. If we believe in this other dimension, we must live in the reality of that.

What changes behaviour?

I have struggled for a number of years with a simple question. What is it that will change human behaviour? What can we do that will convince people that there is a better way to live? Is there any hope for our world? What chance do we have to ask people not to have sex until they are married? Is it just pie in the sky? These are big questions that many have grappled with over the years and at times arrived at some good answers. Education is important. We all need information so that we can make informed choices. Sex education has a vital role to play and we need to ensure that it is the right sort. Education can lead to a better quality of life. But it's not enough.

Peer reinforcement will help, that is, getting the young people into like-minded groups. In this way they will reinforce the positive principles in which they believe. That's why it's important to try and encourage your children to become active members of a church youth group. In doing this they will be amongst like-minded people. It will help . . . but it's not enough.

Fear can and will change human behaviour. It is interesting that Jesus spoke more about hell than heaven. A healthy fear is a good thing. It's for this reason that spelling out some of the potential consequences of sex is important. They are real. Sexually-transmitted diseases can be caught. Young people need to realize this. The evidence, however, shows that fear changes some behaviour but not all. Despite all the education and publicity about AIDS over 50 per cent of sexually active teenagers still do not use a condom. The reason given? They don't think they will contract the disease. Fear has not worked in these cases.

All these things have their place, but the overwhelming reason why people change is because they see that there is a better way to live. And that is our challenge today. It is the challenge for the Church, the individual and the family.

How do we convince young people that they should listen to the things we say? It starts by earning the right to be heard. And the way we do that is we show that there is a better way to live. They will not listen to our advice on sex if we are inconsistent in other areas. These are some of the comments made by young people:

> How can churches serve our generation? By acknowledging that everyone has their faults, by supporting people in crisis without judging, and by facing the issues we deal with every day. Our generation is very practical: show me relevance. Help me deal with career decisions, morality, AIDS, dysfunctional families, substance abuse. *Mary aged 21*

> I used to want to be a super Christian. The reason I stopped pursuing that goal was because I had no role models. All the people from my church are hypocrites. *Mel*

They want reality. And that means living the faith. It means showing that your life is lived by priorities other than worldly ones. If we start doing that, then I believe the tide of opinion can change. People will begin to take note.

Henri Nouwen is a Canadian who had a distinguished teaching career at Notre Dame, Yale and Harvard universities. God then called him to give up his academic career and go to work as a priest among a handicapped community in Toronto. He describes the change as very disconcerting. He moved from an environment were everybody knew of him. He was famous, he had a lot of prestige and he was numbered as one of the successful. He moved to an environment where nobody knew of his academic achievement and even if they did, it meant nothing to them. All of us would find that kind of change hard. And as he began to work with these people, as he washed them, as he sat with them for hours as their bodies writhed in pain, it slowly dawned on him that he'd been living with the wrong priorities. He had been measuring success by the wrong standards. He realized that driving ambition, competition and striving for success were all wrong in the Christian world.

That is not the way Jesus operated and it's not the way that we are meant to. The Church of today does not need success stories; rather it needs people who have the heart of Jesus. He realized that he needed to start living as Jesus lived. From his experience and thinking Henri Nouwen has come up with this definition of success:

> Keep your eyes on the one who refuses to turn stones into bread, jump from great heights or rule with great temporal power. Keep your eyes on the one who says, 'Blessed are the poor, the gentle, those who mourn and those who hunger and thirst for righteousness; blessed are the merciful, the peacemakers and those who are persecuted in the cause of uprightness' . . . Keep your eyes on the one who is poor with the poor, weak with the weak and rejected with the rejected. That one is the source of all peace.[39]

Be brave, be radical

It was a wet, cold and miserable night, but it did not stop the church hall filling up with people. There were balloons on the wall, streamers hanging from the ceiling and a band was on stage playing numbers from the 60s. It was party time. But this was a party with a difference for this was a party for the homeless. A local church had collected over 100 homeless people off the street and brought them up to the hall. Tables were laid out with food fit for a king. Church members served them as they sat down for their food. Then as the band played on one or two got up to dance. Soon a number of them were jigging to the sound of the 60s. Why did they dance? Some danced because they liked the tune, others danced because they were already drunk when they arrived at the party. There were a few, however, who danced because their inner being was touched by the better way. They could sense, almost touch, this better way. And do you know what they sensed from this encounter with the better way? You are valuable and greatly loved. That's why they danced because for the first time in years they could hold their heads up and know dignity and love. That's what the Kingdom of God can do for people. Those are the priorities worth fighting for.

Young people need to be challenged to live out this radical calling. Set the standard for them to follow. Make the work of the Kingdom your priority. Feed the homeless; start projects that will help house them. Get involved in a hospice for those dying of AIDS. Work amongst the handicapped community. Visit the sick and throw parties for the elderly.

Do this and teenagers will begin to believe in the better way. Young people will be challenged by it. They will see that there are different standards and priorities. But above all they will discover that God is real, that He can be known and that He has plans for their lives. Then when they encounter Him and grow to love Him, He will whisper into their hearts and minds that to live by His standards is a better way. And they will listen and they will change because they will believe it.

> Go on then,
> be brave,
> be radical and show the young people that to you . . .
> . . . there is a better way to live.

Notes

1 Norman Vincent Peale, *Power of the Plus Factor*, Mandarin.
2 L. J. Francis and W. Kay, *Moving Currents in Youth Culture*, Lynx, 1995.
3 N. Ford, *The Social-Sexual Lifestyles of Young People in the South-West of England*, University of Exeter, 1991.
4 Government Statistical Service, 1933.
5 Dr P. Dixon, *The Rising Cost of Love*, Hodder & Stoughton, 1995.
6 M. Myers, *Young People: Relationships, Lifestyle and Sexual Attitudes*, Marc Europe and Agape, 1991.
7 S. Strickland, 'Speaking Personally about Teenage Sex', *The Independent*, 21 November 1991.
8 James Ferman, 'Panorama', 27 February 1995.
9 A. Ries and J. Trout, *Positioning: The Battle for your Mind*, New York: McGraw Hill, 1981.
10 A. Carole, *Daily Express*, 7 March 1995, p.20.
11 University of Lancashire Study, 1993.
12 *Independent on Sunday*, 19 January 1992.
13 'Cultural Trends', Policy Studies Institute, *Daily Telegraph*, 20 January 1994.
14 L. Masterman, *Teaching the Media*, Routledge, 1990.
15 Audi.
16 British Telecom.
17 AIDS.
18 Vauxhall.
19 Carling Black Label.
20 James Ferman, 'Panorama', 27 February 1995.
21 Sir Robin Day, *The Listener*, 18 December 1980.
22 R. Joffe, *Vision and Home Video*, March 1980.

23 *The Guardian*, 23 February 1995, p.14.

24 R.G. DeMoss, *Learn to Discern*, Zondervan, 1992.

25 *The Sunday Times*, 10 January 1993.

26 D. Boorstin, *The Image*, New York: Atheneum, 1961.

27 Dr B. Spock, *The Times*, 20 March 1994.

28 *The Guardian*, 7 October 1993, p.21.

29 Dr D. Birch, *The Sunday Times*, 5 January 1992.

30 ibid.

31 S. Chalke, *Lessons in Love*, CARE.

32 R. Lovelace, *Homosexuality: Finding the Way of Truth and Love*,
    Cambridge Papers.

33 M. Joseph, *Aching and a Longing*.

34 Peter Gabriel, *Us*.

35 Madonna, *The Independent*, 18 May 1991.

36 V. Frankl, *Psychotheraphy and Existentialism*, Penguin Books.

37 Henri Nouwen, *Christianity Today*, 3 October 1994.

38 Tom Wolfe, *Time*, 13 February 1980, p.41.

39 Henri Nouwen, *The Path of Peace*, Darton, Longman and Todd,
    1995.